ESL, EFL,
and Bilingual Education

Exploring Historical, Sociocultural, Linguistic, and Instructional Foundations

A volume in
Bilingual Education Series

Series Editor
Liliana Minaya-Rowe, *University of Connecticut*

Research in Bilingual Education

Liliana Minaya-Rowe, Series Editor

ESL, EFL, and Bilingual Education: Exploring Historical, Sociocultural, Linguistic, and Instructional Foundations (2010)
by Lynn W. Zimmerman

Effective Practices in Training Teachers of English Learners (2010)
edited by Liliana Minaya-Rowe

Negotiating Social Contexts: Identities of Biracial College Women (2007)
edited by Andra M. Basu

*Teacher Training and Effective Pedagogy
in the Conext of Student Diversity* (2002)
edited by Liliana Minaya-Rowe

ESL, EFL, and Bilingual Education

Exploring Historical, Sociocultural, Linguistic, and Instructional Foundations

by

Lynn W. Zimmerman
Purdue University Calumet

Information Age Publishing, Inc.
Charlotte, North Carolina • www.infoagepub.com

Library of Congress Cataloging-in-Publication Data

Zimmerman, Lynn W.
  ESL, EFL, and bilingual education : exploring historical, sociocultural, linguistic, and instructional foundations / by Lynn W. Zimmerman.
    p. cm. — (Research in bilingual education)
  Includes bibliographical references.
  ISBN 978-1-61735-031-3 (paperback) — ISBN 978-1-61735-032-0 (hardcover) — ISBN 978-1-61735-033-7 (e-book)
  1. Education, Bilingual—United States. 2. English language—Study and teaching—United States—Foreign speakers. 3. Sociolinguistics—United States. I. Title.
  LC3731.Z54 2010
  370.117'5—dc22

                                            2010012626

Printed in the United States of America

CONTENTS

PART IV:
EFFECTIVELY TEACHING BILINGUAL/ESL/EFL STUDENTS
149

PART I

Historical, Legal, and Political Foundations of Bilingual/ESL Education

OVERVIEW

Give me your tired, your poor,
Your huddled masses yearning to breathe free.
The wretched refuse of your teeming shore,
Send these, the homeless, tempest-tost to me,
I lift my lamp beside the golden door.
—Emma Lazarus

Emma Lazarus' poem is inscribed on the Statue of Liberty which has been a symbol of freedom for over 100 years. Although the United States has welcomed immigrants throughout its history, it has also set obstacles in their way, at least in the way of some immigrants. Laws such as the Naturalization Act of 1790, which stayed on the books until 1952, defined an American citizen as a "free White person." Therefore, from its inception, the United States has placed barriers in the path of immigrants from non-English-speaking countries and from countries where inhabitants are dark-skinned. They have often faced numerous challenges in trying to become part of American society and culture. Many of these barriers have

ESL, EFL, and Bilingual Education: Exploring Historical, Sociocultural, Linguistic, and Instructional Foundations, pp. 1–4
Copyright © 2010 by Information Age Publishing

been created using language, and implemented through education (Spring, 2004).

Even though they were not immigrants to this country, the Naturalization Act of 1790 also applied to Native Americans. Native Americans were not able to become American citizens until 1924. Even though they were not eligible for citizenship, education was provided for Native Americans. However, its primary aims were to train them for vocations and to replace their language and culture with English and the Anglo culture of the United States.

Black Americans by and large were brought to this country as forced immigrants or an "involuntary minority" (Gibson & Ogbu, 1991). They were sold into slavery and formed the basis of the Southern plantation economy. They were denied access to schooling before and after the Civil War. Literacy was used as a tool for denying full citizenship to the freed slaves, because in many states, in order to vote one had to be able to read.

In the late 1800s Chinese immigrants were welcomed to help build the railroads and open up the West; that is, single males were welcomed. The assumption was that they would work and then return to China, not settle in this country. Many Chinese did, in fact, return to China. No education was provided for them and knowledge of English was not deemed necessary, since they were viewed as temporary inhabitants. Finally, "laws such the Naturalization Act of 1870 and the Chinese Exclusion Act of 1882 restricted immigration of Chinese immigrants into the U.S." (Immigration, n.d., para. 6).

During World War II, in order to address the severe shortage of farm workers, the United States and Mexico established the *Bracero* program which brought thousands of Mexicans from their rural communities to work as farm laborers in the US. Because their contracts were written in English, most of the workers did not understand "their full rights and the conditions of employment" (Farmworkers', n.d., para.6). They usually lived in substandard conditions and were often ill-treated. When the program ended in 1964, "the U.S. Department of Labor officer in charge of the program, Lee G. Williams, had described it as a system of 'legalized slavery'" (Farmworker's, n.d., para. 10).

Therefore, the English language has been and continues to be used to erect barriers preventing non-English speakers from participating fully in American life. Lack of knowledge of English can create conditions under which a person's human and civil rights can be abridged. Knowledge of English can create opportunities, and is important for becoming a member of American life and culture. On the other hand, knowledge of English can be misused to try to eliminate a person's connection to their own language and culture. The educational system is often the battleground where these battles are fought.

This set of essays focuses on the background of bilingual and ESL education in the United States, by examining various historical, legal, and political issues that have been and are of importance in this field.

- Chapter 1: "The English Only Movement: The Power to Silence" provides a brief overview of the historical development of bilingual and ESL education in the United States, and specifically focuses on the legal and political issues surrounding the English Only Movement. (Originally published: Zimmerman, L. W. (2007). The English Only Movement: The power to silence. In D. Witkowsky & K. Schuster, *Language in the Land*. Charlotte, NC: Information Age. Reprinted with permission of the editor.)
- Chapter 2: "Bilingual Education as a Manifestation of an Ethic of Caring" provides an overview of bilingual and ESL education in the United States. Supports bilingual education based on the Nel Noddings' notion of an "ethic of caring." (Originally published: Zimmerman, L. (2000). Bilingual education as a manifestation of an ethic of caring. *Educational Horizons, 78*(2), 72-76. Reprinted with permission of the editor.)
- Chapter 3: "Culture of silence: The Complicity of American Education" explores how standardized testing and the No Child Left Behind (NCLB) Act unite to maintain inequality in American society by failing to take into account the diverse backgrounds and diverse learning needs of students in American schools. Grounded in the critical perspectives of Freire, Delpit, and Apple. (Originally published: Zimmerman, L. W. (2007). Culture of silence: The complicity of American education. *Journal of Contemporary Educational Issues, 3*(1), 20-26. Reprinted with permission of the editor.)
- Chapter 4: "Standard American English: Focus on Profanity as a Social Language Issue in the ESL/EFL Classroom" examines standard American English and a form of nonstandard English, profanity, and their roles in society and the classroom. (Portions of this article were originally published as: Zimmerman, L. W. (2007). Reflections on standard English in the EFL classroom. *ELT (English Language Teaching) Journal, 61*(2), 164-166.)

REFERENCES

Farmworkers' Website. (n.d.). *The Bracero Program*. Retrieved from http://www.farmworkers.org/bracerop.html

Gibson, M., & Ogbu, J. (Eds.) (1991). *Minority status and schooling: A comparative study of immigrants and involuntary minorities*. New York, NY: Garland.

Immigration: The living mosaic of people culture and hope. (n.d.) Retrieved November 4, 2008 from http://library.thinkquest.org/20619/Chinese.html

Spring. J. (2004). *American education* (11th ed.). Boston, MA: McGraw-Hill.

CHAPTER 1

THE ENGLISH-ONLY MOVEMENT

The Power to Silence

There are codes or rules for participating in power [and these] rules of the culture of power are a reflection of the rules of the culture of those who have power. (Delpit, 1993, p. 24)

INTRODUCTION

The proponents of a policy of English Only assert that making English the official language of the United States would ensure that all members of this society would have equal opportunities to participate fully in American life and society. I believe, however, that by coercing non-English speakers to have knowledge of English as their only means of participating in American society is an exercise of power by the dominant culture that devalues the minority language and culture, and denies these people equality and human dignity by silencing them. It is not surprising that education is at the center of the struggle between opponents to and proponents of the English Only movement, because this power to silence is especially effective with children, society's most powerless members.

The debate between proponents and opponents of the English Only movement centers on two primary issues, national identity and civil

ESL, EFL, and Bilingual Education: Exploring Historical, Sociocultural, Linguistic, and Instructional Foundations, pp. 5–21

rights. Proponents of the movement argue that they are concerned with maintaining what they see as the "American way of life." Opponents to English Only contend that this movement is an abridgement of civil rights. I suggest that by limiting their argument to political and economic issues, the opponents to English Only are neglecting the more basic issue of exclusionary practices in education, which maintains the oppression of language minorities.

Before presenting my argument that the English Only movement is based on creating and maintaining a power differential through education, I will first explain the ways in which I intend to use the terms "identity" and "power," and how I see them in relation to language issues. Then I will give some historical background on English in the United States, and on language education in the Unites States, focusing on bilingual education. This section will be followed by the arguments put forward by the supporters of English Only, and by those who are against it. Finally, I will examine educational practices in the context of the power, and identity issues involved in the English Only debate.

THE RELATIONSHIP OF IDENTITY
AND POWER TO LANGUAGE ISSUES

Language is essential to the entire range of human interactions, making issues of language extremely complex. Language issues involve collective and individual identities; political, economic, and social rights; power and status with their opportunities for exclusion and inclusion; and issues of choice.

Language issues are embedded in the multi-faceted concept of identity. Identity may be defined as having two main dimensions, collective and individual, each characterized by different elements. Characteristics such as gender; race and/or ethnicity; religion; culture and/or society, are often referred to as collective identity. The second dimension, individual identity, includes characteristics, such as sex, intelligence or charm. This paper will examine individual identity as well as two characteristics of collective identity in relation to language policies, national identity and cultural identity.

National identity is an attempt to unify a population legally, linguistically, culturally, and ideologically. National identity is created by the political structure, which determines what is acceptable or not for the citizens under its control. The dominant culture in a country is often considered to be synonymous with national identity, because, this cultural identity presents what at first seems to be a "coherent unified worldview" which is actually "the ideology of a dominant group or interest" (Martin, 1996,

p. 153). This ideology or worldview may or may not correspond with the cultural identity of all of its people, but "every self-regulating state attempts to socialize the individual in a manner deemed to be consistent with the goals of its political system" (Martin, 1996, p. 153). This socialization is usually accomplished through the use of language. The political structure may even dictate that the population as a whole speak one language. Despite there being a multitude of cultures within the United States, its political structure has historically supported English as the dominant language.

Although a "national" language is an important unifying element and creates "a community of … intercommunicating elite" (Hobsbawn, 1990, p. 59), having a national language has advantages and disadvantages for the populace. In the past, there was little attempt to establish direct communication between the ruled and rulers, who often spoke different languages. The rulers had to use intermediaries to convey their decrees to the populace who had little or no ability to know if they were receiving accurate representations, and did not have the ability to reply back. The use of a national language has the advantage of allowing the populace to have direct communication with the government and makes the government appear to be more accessible to the citizens. On the other hand, the use of a national language can create and maintain the dominance of the power elite, by supporting their language as the only means of official and, consequently, nonofficial communication.

Cultural identity is not necessarily the same as national identity. It is made up of a variety of related patterns of behavior, beliefs, practices, and values that generally exist in a historical context. Family structure can be a characteristic of cultural identity, as can be funeral practices, and religious beliefs. The dominant culture in the United States is the Anglo-American culture, but the population of the nation from its inception has been multicultural, so there are numerous cultural identities within this nation.

One of the principal characteristics of cultural identity is language, which creates a symbol of the unity for the members of the culture, past, present, and future. According to Bunge, it forms a discourse that embodies the "systems of thought and the worldviews" (Crawford, 1992, p. 376) of the culture. This discourse is dialectical in nature. The language is not only shaped by the members of the group, but it also shapes them, by creating, and oftentimes reifying, ideas in words.

In a multicultural society, several discourses exist, but the dominant discourse is the public one, a discourse which confers power in the social arena and access to economic success. Other discourses are usually limited to the private sphere. Although one's primary discourse, the one learned at home, may not be the same as the public discourse, the dominant discourse can be taught to anyone. Despite the complex intertwining of language, culture, identity, and power, it is not necessary that through learning another discourse the individual must reject her home identity and values.

Because identity formation occurs as a result of individuals' interactions with those around them, individual identity is created and maintained by one's national and cultural identities. Identity is created not only by how the individual sees herself, "but also by the image that others recognize in and communicate to [her]" (Arcilla, 1995, p. 160). When there is a difference in how someone sees herself and how others see her, it often causes the individual to change her self-image to adapt to how others see her. If that change causes the individual to form a negative view of herself, a power differential results, which can imprison her in this identity. If a person or group receives negative messages about themselves, whether directly or through omission, they develop "a demeaning picture of themselves" (Taylor, 1994, p. 65). Whether these messages are intentional or not, they still deliver the same message of inferiority. This recognition/ misrecognition by others has a profound effect on how a person or group of people sees themselves, and how their self-concept develops.

Language is one way that this identity is transmitted and communicated to others. Language is equated with thoughts and words are equated with ideas. If someone cannot express herself well, others assume that her thinking is faulty, not her communication patterns. This knowledge that one's very identity is being judged by such standards can have serious effects on a person who is living within another culture. Speakers of languages other than the dominant one often experience feelings of shame, alienation, guilt, fear, hostility, confusion, lack of pride and inadequacy. They often express their experiences with language as being disconcerting, traumatic, and terrorizing. All of these negative emotions and reactions can have a negative effect on that person's self-concept. On the other hand, if one's efforts at communication are met positively, she is able to "develop or maintain a positive concept of self" (Crawford, 1992, p. 345) and experience feelings of acceptance, worth, and higher self-esteem.

In *Teaching to Transgress*, bell hooks (1994) shows the strong link between language and domination. Language is the weapon that the dominant group (the oppressors) use to limit and define, even to shame and humiliate. Establishing a common language, and using it for national communication, especially written communication, makes it seem permanent, and creates a need for literacy in that language. Public education and administrations serve to foster and perpetuate the dominance of the language. On the other hand, learning to speak the dominant language helps the language minority person to gain and reclaim personal power within a context of domination.

A child entering school in the United States who knows no English and has no support at school in his first language is caught in a situation in which his individual and cultural identity make him powerless. Yarborough says that the child quickly begins to believe "that there is something wrong with him because of his language. This misbelief soon spreads to the images he has of his culture, of the history of his people, and of his people themselves" (cited in Crawford, 1992, p. 324). In this way the child's identity is defined and redefined by the use of language, and he is permanently altered by these changes.

Before exploring educational issues further, I would like to look at how English was established as the common language in the United States. The use of English as the dominant language in American education has a historical source, based on the national identity derived from the dominant Anglo-American culture of the United States.

HISTORY OF ENGLISH IN AMERICA

The discussion of English as the official language is not new to this century. In the early days of the European settlement of what later became the United States, many western European languages were spoken, as well as Greek, Arabic, and various African languages, not to mention the languages of the native peoples of this continent. However, when the United States was being formed as a nation, such influential men as John Jay, Benjamin Franklin, and Thomas Jefferson were concerned that American citizens should be English-speaking. They wanted to establish an American society and culture that reflected their own Anglo-Saxon cultural identity. Although English was not declared as the official language of the United States, it became "the de facto language of the laws, the courts, the schools, and the governments of the newly formed states" (Martin, 1996, p. 153) by consensus, coexisting with the other languages of the various groups who settled in the United States.

Throughout the history of the United States there have been communities where the inhabitants spoke languages other than English. In the 19th century many city dwellers were able to receive schooling in their first language. "At the turn of the century, more than 6% of American school children were receiving most or all of their primary education in the German language alone" (Nunberg, 1997, p. 2). Increased industrialization during the nineteenth century presented a need for more workers. This need was filled with increasing numbers of immigrant workers. However, this influx of non-English speaking immigrants created a fear among many Anglo-Americans that the United States was losing its national identity, the monolingual monoculture that was seen as the American ideal. Literacy and education were used to promote this Anglo-American culture.

During the mid- to late-1800s, a number of states passed literacy laws which laid the groundwork for other changes in language policy. Literacy is part of the language issue, because the ability to read and write can impact a person's place and role in society. These laws, requiring literacy in English in order to vote, were a convenient method for abridging the rights of those who were not easily accepted as "American," those who were not Anglo-American. Large numbers of Chinese immigrants were not allowed to vote because of these laws, and the so-called "Jim Crow" laws disenfranchised Black Americans, denying them their full rights as American citizens, even though they were born in this country and were native English speakers (National Education Association, 1999).

Compulsory schooling, which began in the United States in the nineteenth century "as a way of transmitting and maintaining Anglo-American culture and language" (Stein, 1988, p. x) is related to immigration and language issues. Many American citizens saw the waves of immigration of the late nineteenth century and early twentieth century as threats to the Anglo-American way of life. Education was used to socialize immigrants into American culture and society. Immigrant children soon learned that if they wanted to succeed in American society, "they had to anglicize themselves and assimilate into Anglo-American culture" (Stein, 1988, p. 4). This ideology with its emphasis on acculturation and assimilation resulted in "the ability to speak English [being] made a condition for citizenship in 1906, and in 1915 an English-literacy requirement was added" (Nunberg, 1997, p. 7). Anti-German sentiment as a result of America's entry into World War I effectively eliminated German bilingual programs, which served about 600,000 students, and remaining bilingual education programs quickly followed. "Within the space of a few years, 35 states passed laws mandating English-only instruction (Attinasi, 1998, p. 9).

After World War II, the approach to assimilation began to change, but assimilation was still the desired goal. The concept of cultural deprivation, espoused by Judith Krugman (Stein, 1988), a New York City school psychologist, stated that students who performed poorly were not genetically inferior, but were raised in an inferior culture. According to Stein (1988), this ideology "was based on the belief that if immigrants and their families would replace their culture with the American culture, they would succeed in American society" (p. 12). This shift in perspective did serve to focus more attention on the problems these students had in schools, and English as a Second Language (ESL) programs and/or bilingual education programs were instituted in some school systems. However, bilingual education did not make a significant comeback until the 1970s.

Bilingual education, which has had mixed success in the United States, has been at the center of the debate between those who support English Only and those who do not. Whether bilingual education is successful is more an indication of the quality of the various programs than an indication of the effectiveness of bilingual education itself (Zimmerman, 2000). Inadequate funding, lack of qualified teachers, inconsistency of programs, and lack of attention to differences among school districts create problems for bilingual programs. However, well-structured bilingual programs can help Limited English Proficiency (LEP) students be successful students—students who are able to learn academic subjects and be competent in English. Coral Way Elementary School in Dade County, Florida is one model of a successful bilingual program.

In 1962, the Ford Foundation awarded Coral Way Elementary School a grant for a 3-year experimental Spanish-English program. The impetus for this innovative program was the large influx of wealthy and educated Cubans escaping Castro's regime who were interested in dual language literacy for their children. The goal of the program was to educate children from English-speaking homes and from Spanish-speaking homes in a dual language program, so that all the children would be fluent in both languages (Attinasi, 1998). Although it was not without opposition and controversy, this program's success opened the door for bilingual education nationwide (Stein, 1988).

In the wake of the Civil Rights Movement, more attention was given to language minority students. Title VI of the Civil Rights Act of 1964 was intended to end racial segregation in schools. It was also used to address other forms of discrimination which deny individuals opportunities for education and educational achievement.

In a research project conducted in Texas in 1966, Anne Stemmler (as cited in Moraes, 1996) found that Spanish-speaking children were not receiving equal opportunities for education. According to Stemmler, their Spanish language and culture was "often judged irrelevant for academic learning and reading" (Moraes, 1996, p. 46). She also found that many Spanish-speaking students were labeled mentally retarded based on low IQ scores. "However, since IQ tests were written in English, these non-English speaking students were considered deficient learners because their linguistic performance in English was directly connected to levels of intelligence" (Moraes, 1996, p. 46).

In 1967, the Bilingual Education Act (BEA), Title VII of the Elementary and Secondary Education Act passed, making bilingual education an issue of federal policy. Title VII provides funding for teacher training as well as for materials for Transitional Bilingual Education (TBE) programs. Although this act affects all students whose first language is not English, its primary aim was to improve the performance of Hispanic students in school (Stein, 1988). Subsequently, most bilingual education programs have been designed for students whose first language is Spanish.

In addition to legislation, several Supreme Court cases have given support to bilingual programs. The 1974 decision, *Lau v. Nichols*, while not specifically mandating bilingual education, stated "non-English speaking students were entitled to appropriate help in overcoming language barriers" (Attinasi, 1998, p. 9). Opponents to English Only see these court cases as supporting their stance that language issues are civil rights issues.

Especially important in the debate between English Only supporters and those who favor bilingual policies are the language policies of the state of California. According to Attinasi (1998), "California is a test case for the nation, especially regarding language and education" (p. 3). In 1977 California passed legislation providing bilingual language programs for students. However, these programs quickly came under attack from a number of groups, which contended that education should only be provided in English. While steps were being taken to provide language support services for immigrant students, other forces saw these programs as being in opposition to "the American way of life." Although bilingual education continued to be a controversial and hotly debated topic, California supported bilingual education until 1998, when Proposition 227, English for the Children" was passed. Proposition 227 mandates that all instruction be in English and that non-English-speaking students only be allowed a 1-year transition period in sheltered English immersion classes, unless parents apply for special waivers. Proposition 227 has been under attack since its passage, and this 1-year transition period has proven to be a weak point since language acquisition research shows that gaining adequate fluency in a language for academic success can take five or more years. In these 1-year transition programs students focus on language skills rather than content. After exiting the program, they are then expected to catch up on missed content and "make two years of academic progress for every one year of instruction between Grades 1-4" (Mora, 2003, Premature Cries section, para. 4). Students who do not make this progress can be retained. Rather than being a motivator, retention has been shown to result in less engagement with education and increased dropout rates (Mora, 2003). Since the passage of the bill, school systems have struggled with its implementation resulting in a variety of interpretations of the law, including the continuation of some bilingual programs. According to some studies which have been conducted on the effectiveness of Proposition 227, while more students are passing standardized tests, these higher pass rates cannot be attributed solely to the proposition. Other factors, especially the accountability movement, have to be considered (Scully, 2004). Even 6 years after its passage, the ongoing debate over the effectiveness of bilingual education versus English Only education has not been resolved.

THE ENGLISH-ONLY MOVEMENT

The English-Only Movement emerged in the early 1980s as a reaction to bilingualism and bilingual education. With its rhetoric of "national unity, patriotism and fiscal responsibility" (Reuben, 1996, p. 44), English Only is supported by a number of groups such as US English, English First, and the American Ethnic Coalition, as well as being endorsed by groups such as The National Grange, and many individuals. Its two main themes are "to keep America 'American' in the face of large-scale immigration and to speed up the assimilation process for groups which seem to resist assimilation" (Ricento, 1999, p. 2).

Keeping America "American" means to maintain the dominant Anglo-American cultural identity, which includes the English language. S.I. Hayakawa, one of the founders of U.S. English, stated that language is the unifying element that has created American society from "the hodge-podge of nationalities, races, and colors" (Crawford, 1992, p. 94) that make up the United States. Language is considered a crucial part of culture and the proponents of English Only go so far as to say that they want to protect "the nation from possibly losing the English language" (Arzola, 1996, p. 18). Supporters of California's Proposition 227 also used this argument to support their campaign. They said that Prop 227 would provide " 'legal protection' for the language, yet provided no documentation that English is endangered" (Attinasi, 1998, p. 4).

Another argument that proponents of English Only use is that knowledge of English promotes assimilation into American culture. Knowledge of English provides willing and deserving immigrants with the cultural capital needed to become part of American culture. They assert that by not learning English, non-English speakers are being subjected to a form of "cultural apartheid" (National Education Association, 1999, p. 4). They claim that immigrants who cannot communicate in English are being segregated from full participation in American society on the basis of their language. Supporters of English Only think this assimilation is critical if the United States is to maintain its national identity.

There are now at least 28 states that have official English laws and these laws vary from state to state.

Some versions void almost all state and federal laws that require the government to provide services in languages other than English. The services affected include: health, education, and social welfare services; job training and translation assistance to crime victims and witnesses in court and administrative proceedings; voting assistance and ballots; drivers' licensing exams, and AIDS-prevention education (American Civil Liberties Union, 1999, p. 2).

In addition to these state laws, some federal laws have been passed, including an English Only bill in the House (Arzola, 1996, p. 18). There has also been support for an English Only amendment to the Constitution, but opponents have contended that an English Language Amendment would change the nature of the Constitution so that it becomes "a charter of restrictions that limits, rather than protects, individual rights" (American Civil Liberties Union, 1999, p. 1). Opponents of such laws and proposals say that "historically, where such restrictions have been implemented, they have effectively disenfranchised large numbers of immigrants from access to government services, voting, and equal educational opportunities" (Ricento, 1999, p. 2). They suggest that a number of new restrictive welfare laws aimed at immigrants have been sponsored by those who support English Only. Many human rights organizations have filed "floods of amicus briefs with the Supreme Court arguing against " (Reuben, 1996, p. 44) such laws. One such brief was filed on behalf of native Hawaiians. John H. Ishihara, the attorney who filed the amicus brief, said that the purpose of the law was "to achieve a false sense of unity through an apparently homogenous polity by rendering invisible those who do not look and talk like 'Americans'" (Reuben, 1996, p. 44). Some opponents to California's Proposition 227 claim that language is a secondary issue. They assert that the real impetus behind the law is an attempt to suppress Latino culture.

Opponents of English Only tend to focus on the political and economic issues of having English as the official language of the United States. They claim that those who favor it are acting out of general xenophobia, based on false stereotypes, and are attempting "to disenfranchise minority citizens [by promoting] divisiveness and hostility toward those whose first language is not English" (National Education Association, 1999, p. 2). In addition, they say that supporters of English Only are operating "on a totally false premise, i.e., that immigrants are resisting learning English" (Ricento, 1999, p. 6). Padillo (1991) asserts that immigrants are fully aware of how important learning English is

> as a way of improving their socio-economic and geographic mobility in the U.S. In fact, immigrant groups today are probably shifting to English at a faster rate than was true for immigrants from Europe at the turn of the century (p. 38).

The idea of "keeping America 'American'" is contrary to the democratic principles and "the spirit of tolerance and diversity" (American

Civil Liberties Union, 1999, p. 1) upon which America was founded. This contention is not only contradictory, but is also disconnected from the ideals they claim to support. The American Civil Liberties Union argues that "the bond that unites our nation is not linguistic or ethnic homogeneity but a shared commitment to democracy, liberty and equality" (American Civil Liberties Union, 1999, p. 5). The National Education Association states that English Only "ignores our country's civil rights tradition" (National Education Association, 1999, p. 2) by abridging the rights of individuals who are not proficient in English.

Opponents also name specific areas in which English Only would be detrimental to the public sphere, such as health care, government services, voting, judicial procedures, law enforcement, workplace rights, and education.

> Lack of information in non-English languages for pregnant women, for example, will only increase the likelihood of higher medical costs for everyone; lack of multilingual ballots will mean an even greater non-participation rate of eligible voters who are non-English speakers; and abandoning federal support for bilingual education will result in pull-backs on the state level as well. (Ricento, 1999, p. 5)

Opponents to English Only suggest that political and economic power is also at issue. "Some view public support of any type of pluralistic empowerment, especially for the lowest and most silent sectors of society, as politically bold and potentially risky" (Attinasi, 1998, p. 8). They suggest that some supporters of an English Only policy perceive that the existence of large, powerful, unassimilated minority groups threatens the economic and political power of the majority culture. The rising

> number of assertive language minorities in the United States [which has] created "a subeconomy that facilitated linguistic and cultural maintenance." The affirmative use of minority languages and the assertion of gender and racial differences remains a current threat to elites at every national level. (Martin, 1996, p. 153).

The notion that having an English Only policy would promote assimilation is also refuted by its opponents. With this argument, they assert that such an attack on one's cultural identity abridges one's civil rights. "English Only assimilationist policies have tended to undervalue, and hence undermine, their [immigrants'] ancestral languages and cultures, ultimately impeding the assimilation process" (Ricento, 1999, p. 4). However, this attack on cultural identity does more than abridge civil rights as is made clear when examining the issue of education.

EDUCATION AND LANGUAGE POLICIES

One of the primary areas of difference between opponents and proponents of English Only is education. Proponents of English Only see education as a means of transmitting Anglo-American culture and values, with little or no regard for the complexity of the individual student's experiences, abilities, or needs. Former Senator Robert Dole, a supporter of English Only, encapsulates the movement's views when he says that

> schools should provide the language classes our immigrants and their families need, as long as their purpose is the teaching of English ... But we must stop the practice of multilingual education as a means of instilling ethnic pride or as therapy for low self-esteem or out of elitist guilt over a culture built on the traditions of the West (National Education Association, 1999, p. 1).

However, as has been demonstrated by the continuing controversy over Proposition 227 in California, such an oversimplification of the issues of language learning denies the reality facing English language learners. Variations in program implementation and inconsistencies in the interpretation of the proposition's requirements highlight the complexities of English language education. Such a generalization also ignores the difficulties and challenges that many of these students face.

Many of the non-English speaking students coming into American schools today have had little or no education in their country of origin. Low levels of native language literacy impacts their evaluation, placement, and instruction after they have enrolled in American schools. In addition to these educational short-comings, students may have a variety of post-traumatic conditions created by physical and psychological trauma in their home country (Smith-Davis, 2004). The parents of these children are also often experiencing stress that affects their involvement with their children's education. An inability to communicate with school is only one of the problems facing these parents. They may be experiencing posttraumatic stress,

> immigration stress (losses of familiar support systems and coping resources), and acculturative stress (learning to live within an entirely new society; loss of identity). Cultural variations in childcare and child rearing are often poorly understood by school personnel, and many parents exhibit fear of and reluctance to accept interventions, treatments, and assistive devices. (Smith-Davis, 2004, p. 3)

Cultural differences in handling psychological stressors, as well as differences in response patterns and learning styles can also affect the child's and parent's interactions with school personnel.

Opponents of English Only generally support bilingual education, asserting that it enhances a child's ability to learn English, and "engenders a positive self-image and self-respect by validating the child's native language and culture" American Civil Liberties Union, 1999, p. 4) and, according to Gaarder (as cited in Crawford, 1992), by providing a "strong and mutually reinforcing relationship between the home and the school" (p. 326). Lisa Delpit (1993) offers theoretical support for these beliefs when she states that language acquisition is as much an affective as a cognitive process. If someone must constantly monitor her speech, she is likely to either lapse into silence or speak only in the language with which she is comfortable. Being forced to give up one's native language can result in

> a severe loss of self-esteem and alienation from society. When immigrants attempt to lose all traces of their native language and culture, the result may be the loss of their identity with no real feeling of host-culture identity to replace it, leading to the undesirable condition of marginality. (Padilla, 1991, p. 38).

A good grounding in their home culture and language can help children to develop a strong, individual identity upon which to build their collective identity. The "Native American Language Act" states that there has been

> convincing evidence that student achievement and performance, community and school pride, and educational opportunities is clearly and directly tied to respect for, and support of, the first language of the child or student. (Crawford, 1992, p. 155)

When the child's first language is supported and valued, the child is able to stay in touch with the voices of his or her personal history, enabling the development of a cultural identity that is a healthy blend of home culture and the majority culture. Studies by Cummins (1985) and Danesi (1986) have found that when students retain their first language, they not only develop positive attitudes and have enhanced self-esteem, but they also found that their English-language performance is comparable with students in English-only classes, and they tend to perform better in other curriculum areas than those students (Baker, 1993).

However, many language minority students do not benefit from either bilingual education or adequate English education, resulting in disproportionately large high school dropout rates among these students. "High-quality bilingual education programs could promote higher levels of academic achievement and language proficiency in both languages, as well as more positive psychosocial outcomes" (Padilla, 1991, p. 38) resulting in higher student achievement and lower dropout rates.

If English Only were to become the official policy of the United States, it would affect the most powerless members of society most of all, children. Many of the proposed laws specifically prohibit the use of any language besides English in public institutions, including schools. Therefore, if English Only were adopted, all instruction in all public schools must be in English. There would be no bilingual programs to help ease students into the English mainstream. There would be no reading materials to help support their learning. There would be no teachers who speak their language. There would be no support for these students in their own languages in schools. Proponents of English Only expect language minority students to "sink or swim" in English, but provide very little financial or political support to assist them in learning English. This insistence on the learning of English without adequate support systems is an exercise of power by the majority English-speaking culture.

CONCLUSION

Power in and of itself is a positive force within a culture and society. Hannah Arendt (1958) asserts that "power preserves the public realm and the space of appearance" (p. 204) by creating a tension that holds the "web of relationships" that is society together. It is the imbalance of power that creates the negative force. According to Michael Lerner (1996), one of the ways in which those in power maintain this imbalance in their favor is by keeping others from arenas in which they might experience power or seem powerful. From its inception, the United States has been dominated by the Anglo-American culture. This monoculturalism has granted privileges and power to one segment of the population, usually at the expense of other cultural groups in this society. Not only are the other groups denied power, but they are denied access to power through denial of privileges and abridgement of rights.

Access to power in the United States is often granted through knowledge of the English language. Members of the majority culture in the United States, those who have power, rely on the "linguistic forms, communication strategies, and presentation of self" (Delpit, 1993, p. 25) that is shaped by their use of the English language and the Anglo-American culture on which it is based. Delpit (1993) also suggests that those who have "power are frequently least aware of its existence" (p. 26) so that those for whom English is their primary language often do not realize that there is a power imbalance between them and those who do not speak English. However, people who "succeed" in American society are those who acquire this culture—or become assimilated—and the power derived from this acculturation and assimilation implies that the minority language and culture is inferior. The power differential between the dominant and subordinate cultures is increased as the immigrant's power over his/her own language and culture is diminished. Most immigrants realize that this power differential exists and realize that learning English is one way to lessen it.

The English-Only Movement aims toward an American culture that excludes a large number of its residents unless they learn English—in effect, the aim is to silence them. I believe that American culture can confer equality and human dignity on all of its residents by creating a public sphere in which minority languages and cultures are valued as equal to the majority language and culture. While it is important that students gain a useful knowledge of the language of power, this acquisition of English should not be at the expense of their own language and culture. It is important that children be well-grounded in their own code and realize its value; then children can create an individual identity that ensures them membership in their home culture and in the majority culture. Recognition of the multicultural aspects of American society not only allows non-English speakers to preserve their identities and self-images, but also encourages English only speakers to learn multiple perspectives from them and, perhaps, create a more authentic identity for themselves as part of the greater American culture, giving voice to all aspects of American culture.

REFERENCES

Attinasi, J. J. (1998). English Only for California: Children and the aftermath of Proposition 227. *Education, 119*(2), 263-294. Retrieved June 2, 2004 from *EBSCOhost* [online].

American Civil Liberties Union. (1999). *English only.* Retrieved August 25, 1999 from http://www.eff.org/pub/CAF/civil-liberty/english-only.aclu

Arcilla, R. V. (1995). For the stranger in my home: Self-knowledge, cultural recognition, and philosophy of education. In W. Kohli (Ed.), *Critical conversations in philosophy of education* (pp. 159-172). New York: Routledge.

Arendt, H. (1958). *The human condition.* Chicago: University of Chicago Press.

Arzola, F., Jr. (1996). 'Pro-Life' agendas often are dressed in bigotry. *National Catholic Reporter, 32*(40), 18-21. Retrieved August 24, 1999 from *MasterFILE Premier* [online].

Baker, C. (1993). *Foundations of bilingual education and bilingualism.* Philadelphia: Multilingual Matters.

Crawford, J. (1992). *Hold your tongue: Bilingualism and the politics of English Only.* Reading, MA: Addison-Wesley.

Delpit, L. (1993). *Other people's children: Cultural conflict in the classroom*. New York: The New Press.

Hobsbawn, E. J. (1990). *Nations and nationalism since 1780*. New York: Cambridge University Press.

Hooks, B. (1994). *Teaching to transgress: Education as the practice of freedom*. New York: Routledge.

Lerner, M. (1996). *The politics of meaning: Restoring hope and possibility in an age of cynicism*. Reading, MA: Addison-Wesley.

Martin, J. H. (1996). The question of English Only: Miguel Gonzalez Pando's The Great America Justice Game. *Bilingual Review, 21*, 153. Retrieved August 24, 1999 from *MasterFILE Premier* [online].

Mora, J. K. (2003). Status of bilingual education in the post-227 era. Retrieved September 16, 2003 from http://coe.sdsu.edu/people/jmora/LingRights.htm

Moraes, M. (1996). *Bilingual education: A dialogue with the Bakhtin circle*. New York: SUNY Press.

National Education Association. (1999). The debate over English Only. *NEA*. Retrieved August 25, 1999 from http://www.nea.org/society/engonly.html

Nunberg, G. (1997). Lingo jingo: English Only and the new nativism. *The American Prospect, 40*. Retrieved October 23, 1998 from *Infotrac* [online].

Padilla, A. M. (1999). English Only vs. bilingual education: Ensuring a language-competent society. *Journal of Education, 173*(2), 38-51. Retrieved August 24, 1999 from *MasterFILE Premier* [online].

Reuben, R. C. (1996). Whose language is it? *ABA Journal, 82*, 44. Retrieved August 24, 1999 from *MasterFILE Premier* [online].

Ricento, T. (1999). A brief history of language restrictionism in the United States. Retrieved August 27, 1999 from http://www.ncbe.gwu.edu/miscpubs/tesol/official/restrictionism.htm

Scully, J. M. (2004). *After Prop. 227: How non-English speakers are faring in school*. Retrieved June 17, 2004 from http://www.recordnet.com/articlelink/041804/news/articles/041804-gn-1.php

Smith-Davis, J. (2004). The new immigrant students need more than ESL. *Education Digest, 69*(8), 21-26. Retrieved June 2, 2004 from *EBSCOhost* [online].

Stein, C. B., Jr. (1988). *Sink or swim: The politics of bilingual education*. New York: Praeger.

Taylor, C. (1994). *Multiculturalism: Examining the politics of recognition*. Princeton, NJ: Princeton University Press.

Zimmerman, L. W. (2000). Bilingual education as a manifestation of an ethic of caring. *Educational Horizons, 78*(2), 120-124.

REFLECTION QUESTIONS

1. From the standpoint of education, what are advantages and disadvantages to an English Only Policy?

2. What is the "American way of life?" How important is the English language to "supporting the American way of life"?

3. What ethical, social, economic, or legal implications do you see for education with an English Only Policy?

FOLLOW-UP ACTIVITIES

1. Research recent national and state legislation about English Only.
2. Follow-up on California's Prop 227. What have been the effects of this legislation on ELLs?

FURTHER READING

- Jines, T., & Fuller, M. (2003). *Teaching Hispanic children.* Boston, MA: Allyn & Bacon.
- Rodriguez, R. (1982). *Hunger of memory: The education of Richard Rodriguez.* New York, NY: Bantam.
- The Center for Applied Linguistics at http://www.cal.org

CHAPTER 2

BILINGUAL EDUCATION AS A MANIFESTATION OF AN ETHIC OF CARING

INTRODUCTION

Nel Noddings (1993, 1994, 1995b) believes that educators and education have an obligation to adopt an "ethic of caring" in educating young people in America today. She advocates an "ethic of caring," because education is more than training the intellect. Education should also teach students how to understand themselves and others so they can establish authentic relationships with those around them. An authentic relationship is one in which the involved parties can and want to acknowledge and respond to one another's need for care with caring. Noddings suggests that if educators adopt an ethic of caring, many aspects of schooling would change. If American education were based on an ethic of caring, bilingual education programs would be in place in every school district that has non-English-speaking children in it.

In order to demonstrate that an ethic of caring supports bilingual education programs, I first establish a background against which to view bilingual education by looking at language in American society. Then I briefly outline the history of education in America as it relates to assimilation before defining what bilingual education means today and the various

ESL, EFL, and Bilingual Education: Exploring Historical, Sociocultural, Linguistic, and Instructional Foundations, pp. 23–31
Copyright © 2010 by Information Age Publishing

23

forms it can take. Finally, I describe how bilingual education is a manifestation of an ethic of caring.

LANGUAGE AND AMERICAN SOCIETY

Language is a primary characteristic of cultural identity. "Language is not merely seen as a means of communication but as an expression of one's culture and history" (Steiner, 1995, p. 308). English is American society's majority language, the language in which government is run, business is conducted, and schools are taught. However, modern American society is multicultural and many of the cultures that make up this society have different linguistic backgrounds.

American culture has been traditionally Anglocentric and monolingual because most of the settlers who formed what became the United States came from a common culture, that of the British Isles, particularly England. As settlers from other parts of Europe came to America, many learned English and adopted the Anglo-American culture as their own.

Because of this English-only tradition, many "native" Americans do not see the need for multilingualism in this country, and "the use of other languages by various minorities" (Nunberg, 1997, p. 7) has been handled by maintaining an English-only stance. This monolingualism creates a distinct disadvantage for many people in American society. This stance is fostered by school systems that do not accommodate any language other than English.

EDUCATION AND ASSIMILATION IN THE UNITED STATES

Compulsory schooling was begun in the United States in the nineteenth century as a way of transmitting and maintaining Anglo-American culture and language (Stein, 1988). Educators believed that proficiency in two languages was not possible, so educational policymakers declared that students should learn English only. Most schools practiced submersion in English-only classes and aimed at assimilation into the Anglo-American culture. Immigrant children usually were not promoted until they learned English and were often labeled "retarded." Students were often punished for using their first languages at any time on school property. In addition, the general attitude was that education was wasted on these children because they were destined for low-status jobs. All this contributed to high drop-out rates among immigrant children, creating a self-fulfilling prophecy of low school and work performance. Although social reformers such as Jane Addams decried these practices, immigrant children soon learned that in order to succeed in American society, they had to anglicize themselves and assimilate into the Anglo-American culture (Stein, 1988). Nunberg (1997) explains:

> The ability to speak English was made a condition for citizenship in 1906, and in 1915 an English-literacy requirement was added. The justification provided for these measures was a peculiar doctrine about the connection between language and political thought, which held that speaking a foreign language was inimical to grasping the fundamental concepts of democratic society (p. 7).

After World War II, the approach to assimilation began to change, but assimilation was still the desired goal. According to Stein (1988), in 1955, Judith Krugman, a New York City school psychologist, introduced the concept of cultural deprivation. She said that minority students performed poorly, not because they were genetically inferior, but because they were reared in an inferior culture. If they and their families would replace their culture with the American culture, they would succeed in American society. This shift in perspective did focus more attention on the problems these students had in schools, and ESL (English as a Second Language) programs were instituted in many school systems.

Many contemporary opponents to bilingual education believe that it undermines "the national unity that is reflected in a common core of public school values" (Stein, 1988, p. 12) and an English-only curriculum. They believe that bilingual education slows down a student's acculturation, creating disunity and disharmony among ethnic groups rather than the unity that assimilation implies. The assumption is that there is an immutable set of common American values that can be understood and internalized only if the student is fluent in the language of the Angle-American culture from which these values came. By accepting this language and set of values, the student will rid herself or himself of the differences that prevent his or her becoming "truly American."

This emphasis on assimilation is related to what Lisa Delpit (1995) calls the "culture of power." In order to assimilate into American society, these students learn the "linguistic terms, communication strategies, and presentations of self" (Delpit, 1995, p. 25) of the majority culture, usually at the expense of their home culture. Jane Roland Martin (as cited in Weiler, 2001) states that students have been encouraged to cast "off the attitudes and values, the patterns of thought and action associated with" (p. 21) their home cultures and to embrace those of the "more superior" majority culture. More insidiously, there is a hidden curriculum that devalues any culture except the majority culture. This process of assimilation and devaluation often creates a person who has a distorted sense of identity and does not fit into either culture. The successful "assimilator" may be successful according to the terms of the majority culture, but often has unresolved conflicts and doubts about his or her identity, or "authentic self," as Charles Taylor calls it (as cited in Kohli, 1995).

BILINGUAL EDUCATION

Bilingual education has become an important issue in the United States because of the increasing numbers of immigrants from non-English-speaking countries. Bilingual education does not have a national curriculum or structure and there is a range of programs that fall under the heading of bilingual education. It ranges from submersion (sink or swim), in which the student is taught completely in English, to separatist, in which the student learns in his or her first language and little emphasis is placed on learning English skills. A transitional program is one in which the students have classes in their first language while learning English. They are put into mainstream classes as quickly as their English skills allow (Baker, 1993). Most programs in the United States today are a form of submersion program. Guilford County Schools, in North Carolina, uses a modified submersion program in which the students are mainstreamed in academic classes, but pulled out for one or more periods a day (depending on their English proficiency) for sheltered English instruction (English for Speakers of Other Languages—ESOL).

Bilingual programs have had mixed success in the United States. This is more an indication of the quality of the various programs than an indication of the effectiveness of bilingual education. Well-structured bilingual education programs should help students of limited English proficiency become successful students, students who are able to learn academic subjects speak English competently without sacrificing their home languages or cultures. These students are able to maintain cultural identities while attaining a rightful place in American society.

Some opponents of bilingual education claim that it fosters social and economic divisions that deny equality to language-minority groups by denying students the same education that "native" American students receive. Many, including some Hispanics, feel that language, culture, and ethnicity are best taught in the home and church, and that the public schools' main focus should be to prepare students for life in American society (Zuckerman, 1998). Opponents often cite research that indicates that bilingual education is not as effective as an English-only curriculum. They argue that bilingual education, holding students back from learning English effectively, will hurt their prospects for college and work. Students must be proficient in English if they intend to go to college, because American universities teach in English only. Likewise, most employers expect their employees to be fluent in English (Zuckerman, 1998).

BILINGUAL EDUCATION AS A MANIFESTATION OF AN ETHIC OF CARING

In the late twentieth century in the United States this English-only model will not work. The American economic structure is changing as it embraces the global economy. Subsequently, American workplaces and American work forces are changing. Immigration from all parts of the world has made the United States one of most culturally diverse countries in the world, creating an American society and American culture in transition. The image of what an American is is changing, so ideologies must change, too (Toms & Hobbs, 1997). A new educational model must be developed that is based on caring for the individual's growth and development, rather than on fear or on an economic imperative. Supporters of bilingual education believe that well-structured bilingual programs are an important piece of this model.

I suggest that an "ethic of caring" supports bilingual education in schools. As Noddings says, "From the perspective of caring, the growth of those cared for is a matter of central importance" (Noddings, 1994, p. 175). How better to support a child's growth than by recognizing where that child has come from, and by fostering and encouraging his or her growth from this point? An effective bilingual program will produce students who are fluent in their first language and English and proficient in curricular areas. A good bilingual program should also unify "majority and language minority students in integrated curricular settings in which both languages and cultures" (Stein, 1988, p. 12) are valued. All students should be taught that there is more than one "right" way to talk and that "different language forms are appropriate in different contexts" (Delpit, 1998, p. 20). Bilingual education based on an ethic of caring would promote true dialogue among all students and among students and teachers. According to Noddings (1994), "Dialogue provides information about the participants, supports the relationship, induces further thought and reflection, and contributes to the communicative competence of its participants" (p. 141). Noddings (1994) also stresses the importance of students engaging in "real conversations with adults … in which all partners speak, listen, and respond to one another." (p. 113). In order for teachers and students to engage in such conversations, they must first be able to speak the same language. Bilingual education programs would provide teachers who could have conversations with their students.

Delpit (1998) says that "the linguistic form a student brings to school is intimately connected with loved ones, community and personal identity" (p. 19). Therefore, if the school and teachers support and value the child's first language, the child is allowed to stay in touch with the voices of her or his personal history and is able to develop a cultural identity that is a healthy blend of home culture and the majority culture. Parents and teachers can show caring by "providing carefully for the steady growth of the children in their charge" (Noddings, 1995b, p. 24). The validity of this notion is supported by research data.

Studies by Cummins and Danesi (1990) have found that when students retain their first language, they develop positive attitudes and enhanced self-esteem. Their English-language performance is comparable with mainstreamed students and they tend to perform better in other curriculum areas than mainstreamed students (Baker, 1993).

An effective bilingual program offers the students the opportunity to learn English in a structured environment. They quickly learn social vocabulary, and then can take more time to master academic vocabulary. This helps create a "more natural transition into learning in English" (Glover, 1998, p. 85). Learning academic work in their own language allows limited English-proficiency students to concentrate on the academic concepts being taught without having to deal with the complexities of another language (Glover, 1998). Students avoid the stress of being in a class in which they can understand only a fraction of what is being said. When they go to their English language classes, they will be better able to concentrate on that subject as well as all the others they are taking. As they are eased into English only classes, they will have the confidence to use their English skills. It also offers support to those students who have trouble mastering English.

This goes beyond ensuring that students are comfortable in school. As Noddings contends, "Caring implies a continuous search for competence.... It demonstrates respect for the full range of human talents" (Noddings, 1995a, p. 367). The student who is comfortable in the school situation feels a lower level of stress and is able to develop competence in his or her schoolwork confidently.

The program should also strive to connect with the child's community and preserve and respect the child's home language and culture. The student should be able to connect what is learned in the classroom to home culture to avoid any alienation. This can be accomplished by developing the program "in consultation with adults who share their culture" (Delpit, 1995, p. 45).

All students and their parents should feel a part of the school community. Noddings says that one of the ways parents and teachers can show caring for their students is "by cooperating in children's activities" (Noddings, 1995b, p. 24). An effective bilingual program allows parents of limited-English-proficiency students to stay better connected to their schoolwork. They can communicate easily with the teachers and they are better able to help their children with homework. As with any student, it is important that parents of a limited-English-proficiency student participate as part of their child's educational team (van Slambourk, 1998). In English-only programs, parents and students often feel alienated from the school. As the students struggle with the complexities of survival in the majority culture, they often become alienated from home cultures and families. The "connectedness" offered by bilingual programs can reduce such alienation.

In addition, studies done by Swain (1972) and Doyle et al. (1978) indicate that bilingual children tend to have larger vocabularies than monolingual children and to be more flexible and creative in their language usage (as cited in Baker, 1993). These and other studies from the 1970s and 1980s "documented the enhancing and positive effects of bilingualism on a variety of cognitive performance measures, metalinguistic attributes, divergent thinking, and creativity" (Soto, 1997, p. 4). These results suggest that all students would benefit from learning a second language, even those whose first language is English.

If the purpose of education is to teach English, bilingual education has no place in the educational system. However, according to Noddings (1994), education based on an ethic of caring strives "to produce acceptable persons—persons who will support worthy institutions, live compassionately, work productively but not obsessively, care for older and younger generations, be admired, trusted, and respected" (p. 176) no matter what their backgrounds. Therefore, if the purpose of education is to educate the entire student, bilingual education is necessary.

CONCLUSION

An "ethic of caring" in education assumes that every child in the United States has the right to an education that affirms children's identity while preparing them to take their places in American society. Often this right is denied or abridged for the child who comes from a minority culture, especially one whose first language is not English. American education is structured around preparing students to take their places in society with little regard for where students have come from culturally. Bilingual education can be the bridge between the socialization offered by schools and the cultural-identity formation of language minority students. The person who is bilingual has the security of a cultural identity, while English provides the security of being part of the larger American society.

In *Pedagogy of the Oppressed*, Paolo Freire (1970) says, "The pursuit of full humanity cannot be carried out in isolation or individualism, but only in fellowship and solidarity; therefore it cannot unfold in the antagonistic relations between oppressors and oppressed" (p. 66). In order for all people in America to become part of American society, the oppressive aspects of the Anglocentric culture of the past must be abandoned for a new model that validates all the cultures within this diverse society. An ethic of caring in education can be the basis for that model.

REFERENCES

Baker, C. (1993). *Foundations of bilingual education and bilingualism.* Philadelphia: Multilingual Matters.

Cummins, J., & Danesi, M. (1990). *Heritage languages: The development and denial of Canada's linguistic resources.* Toronto, Ontario, Canada: Garamond Press.

Delpit, L. (1995). *Other people's children: Cultural conflict in the classroom.* New York: The New Press.

Delpit, L. (1998). What should teachers do? Ebonics and culturally responsive education. In T. Perry & L. Delpit (Eds.), *The real Ebonics debate: Power, language, and the education of African-American children* (pp. 17-26). Boston: Beacon Press.

Freire, P. (1970). *Pedagogy of the oppressed.* New York: Continuum.

Glover, P. (1998). Class act: A teacher's view. *Christian Science Monitor, 11*, 85.

Kohli, W. (Ed.). (1995). *Critical conversations in philosophy of education.* New York: Routledge.

Noddings, N. (1993). An ethic of caring and its implications for instructional arrangements. In L. Stone (Ed.), *The education feminism reader* (pp. 171-183). New York: Routledge.

Noddings, N. (1994). Conversation as moral education. *Journal of Moral Education, 23*(2), 107-118.

Noddings, N. (1995a). A morally defensible mission for schools in the 21st century. *Phi Delta Kappan, 76*(5), 365-369.

Noddings, N. (1995b). Teaching themes of caring. *Education Digest, 61*(3), 24-29.

Nunberg, G. (1997). Lingo jingo: English Only and the new nativism. *The American Prospect, 40.* Retrieved October 23, 1998 from *Infotrac* [online].

Soto, L. D. (1997). *Language, culture, and power: Bilingual families and the struggle for quality education.* Albany, NY: SUNY Press.

Stein, C. B., Jr. (1988). *Sink or swim: The politics of bilingual education.* New York: Praeger.

Steiner, J. (1995). *European democracies.* New York: Longman.

Toms, F., & Hobbs. A. (1997). *Who are we? Building a knowledge base about the different ethnic, racial, and cultural groups in America.* Forestville, CT: Diverse Books.

van Slambrouck, P. (1998). California educators struggle with end of bilingual education. *Christian Science Monitor, 10*, 1.

Weiler, K. (2001). *Feminist engagements.* New York: Routledge.

Zuckerman, M. B. (1998). The facts of life in America. *U.S. News and World Report, 124*(20), 68.

REFLECTION QUESTIONS

1. From the standpoint of education, what are advantages and disadvantages of bilingual education?
2. How can we create equitable education for all children regardless of their language?
3. How do you see the intersection of language, culture, and identity?

FOLLOW-UP ACTIVITIES

1. Investigate if bilingual programs are offered in your local schools. If they are, how are they managed? If not, what programs are in place for ESL students?
2. Talk to someone for whom English is not their first language about their educational experiences.

FURTHER READING

*   Espinoza-Herold, M. (2003). *Issues in Latino education: Race, school culture, and the politics of academic success*. Boston, MA: Allyn & Bacon.
*   Moraes, M. (1996). *Bilingual education: A dialogue with the Bakhtin Circle*. Albany, NY: SUNY Press.
*   Noddings, N. (1984). *Caring: A feminine approach to ethics and moral education*. Berkeley, CA: University of California Press.

CHAPTER 3

CULTURE OF SILENCE

The Complicity of American Education

INTRODUCTION

Although American education claims equality for all students, it is complicit in the inequalities and inequities in American society by creating a "culture of silence" (Freire, 1970) in a number of ways. This article focuses on two aspects of American education and how they unite to maintain inequality in American society—standardized testing and the No Child Left Behind (NCLB) Act. No Child Left Behind mandates testing of students in order to hold schools accountable for a standard quality of education. However, implementation of NCLB has shown that this rigid accountability system has failed to take into account the diverse backgrounds and diverse learning needs of students in American schools, thereby contributing to the "culture of silence."

FREEDOM, POWER, AND EDUCATION

Paulo Freire (1970), a Brazilian educator and social activist, contended that education is an important force in creating and maintaining the status quo in a society. Depending on the way in which the power structures

ESL, EFL, and Bilingual Education: Exploring Historical, Sociocultural, Linguistic, and Instructional Foundations, pp. 33–41
Copyright © 2010 by Information Age Publishing

of the dominant culture are set up, education can be used to oppress and maintain oppression, or it can be liberatory. In a society in which the dominant power structure oppresses a segment or segments of the population, a passive education is created, an education that prevents the development of "the critical consciousness which would result in their intervention in the world as transformers of the world" (Freire, 1970, p. 54). This type of education serves to make the oppressed even more passive and adaptable to their world of oppression, creating a "culture of silence" in which the oppressed accepts and even helps maintain the status quo. Liberatory education, on the other hand, creates a critical consciousness which liberates not only the oppressed, but the oppressor as well, creating a society in which all members are equally responsible and equally empowered.

Freire (1970) places much of the responsibility for oppression and the freedom from oppression on the educational system. Education in the United States is largely based on what Freire (1970) refers to as the "banking" concept. Teachers deposit information into students' heads. This type of passive education does not "develop the critical consciousness which would result in [the oppressed's] intervention in the world as transformers of the world" (Freire, 1970, p. 54). Instead it serves to make them even more passive and adaptable to their world of oppression. Critical consciousness, on the other hand, is the awareness and action necessary to affect social change, engendering self-affirmation even for those who are trapped in a "culture of silence," those who are kept in ignorance by "economic, social, and political domination" (Freire, 1970, p. 12). Myths are often used to reify this reality. In the United States, myths such as "the value of hard work", "the classless society," and "there's enough for everyone", have been promulgated so that those in power can maintain their power over those who do not benefit from the American system.

In her examination of educational practices, Lisa Delpit (1993) refers to the role of power in the educational system and how it creates a "silenced dialogue." Power is enacted in the classroom through the teacher, the textbooks, the curriculum, and legislation that affects schools. A "culture of power" is created which has codes and rules that are based on the dominant culture, the culture in power. The children who are part of that culture have an immediate advantage in the educational arena, because they have the "cultural capital" needed for success. They understand the stated and unstated rules of being in this group or society. Ways of communicating, dressing, and interacting contribute to these rules, this "cultural capital." Delpit (1993) asserts that the dominant culture strives to maintain the status quo by keeping knowledge of the "cultural capital" from oppressed groups, denying them opportunities to be successful in society, opportunities to gain power. Delpit (1993) contends that these rules should be taught to students who do not grow up as part of the dominant society. In this way they can gain their freedom, overcome oppression, gain power, and make their place within society.

In his analysis of the interplay of education and power in Western countries, Michael Apple (1995) says that "the educational and cultural system is an exceptionally important element in the maintenance of existing relations of domination and exploitation in these societies" (p. 9). He cautions, however, that while schools play an important role, they are "part of a larger framework of social relations that are structurally exploitative" (p. 9). He cites research which suggests that even if schools are changed so that opportunities for achievement are equalized, that inequities in society would still exist, undermining any benefits gained by those who might otherwise benefit from theses educational changes. He asserts that despite school being embedded in the societal framework, that their role cannot be ignored. Schools replicate and reproduce the inequalities and inequities in society.

However, the existing educational system has helped create a society in which social inequalities exist. All students are allowed, even required to attend school. American tax dollars pay for free schooling for all children, so most American students attend public schools. This does not mean that all of these schools are equal. The type of school one attends and the type and quality of education one receives is often determined by one's (supposedly nonexistent) social class. In a study by Jean Anyon (1980) in the 1978-1979 school year, the findings were that there are indeed differences in the way that children are taught. She found that although there are similarities among schools, students are usually taught in the way that will prepare them for life in their social class from which they came. In her conclusion, Anyon (1980) says that a child's school experience is designed to prepare him or her in order to "reproduce this system of relations in society" (p. 90).

Apple (1995) supports Anyon's conclusion by referencing the work of allocation theorists. They assert that school serves as a sorting and sifting device which prepares people for their "proper" place in the work and economic environment. Apple (1995) goes further with his analysis and says that the hidden curriculum in schools also plays a part by going beyond the teaching skills that are deemed "appropriate" for one's station in life, but also by mirroring "the personality and dispositional traits that these students will 'require' later on when they join the labor market" (p. 62). American schools are largely focused on individual work and achievement, which prepares students for the world of work, which also defines a person's place in a society which is stratified by economics and power.

Delpit (1993) concedes the complexity of the power issues in education. There are those who overtly wield power, and those who have power indirectly as a result of being members of the dominant group. These people often do not recognize that a power differential exists and their role in creating a "silenced dialogue." Rather than engaging in direct interactions which recognize power differentials, indirect interactions occur which de-emphasize power and create miscommunication and alienation. In the school setting this plays out when a teacher expresses herself indirectly to a child who needs explicit directions and instructions in how to operate in a different classroom culture. Delpit (1993) reminds her readers that "to act as if power does not exist is to ensure that the power status quo remains the same" (p. 24). To initiate true dialogue power issues must be directly confronted.

Marcia Moraes (1996), who thinks that teachers should be taught that teaching is a political act, argues that educators should develop a dialogic-critical pedagogy in which not only the oppressed become aware and take action, but also the oppressor. She says that the education of the oppressor has been such that they do not see their behavior as oppression, but as normal. They do not realize the ways in which they themselves are oppressed. If they can see and accept their own privilege, they can then transform "into social agents who can change the existing social inequalities and ideologies that constrain their own existence" (Moraes, 1996, p. 116) and that of others.

Teacher education programs do little to prepare teachers for working with students from minority cultures and for teaching them about their own role in the oppressive society. Teachers should do more than support the hidden curriculum and instill "cultural capital" in their students. It is important to build on what students do know rather that focusing on what they do not know. They need to see what the student brings with them as a result of growing up in a different culture.

Despite evidence that alternative methods of teaching and assessment are more effective than the traditional pedagogies, teacher education's focus is still that "teachers learn that one kind of methodology is good for all students" (Moraes, 1996, p. 125). Moraes (1996) advocates that this type of pedagogy be abandoned and that "a dialogical-critical pedagogy [which] perceives students as dynamic and active people who are growing in perspectives within the construction of knowledge" (p. 131) be adopted. Rather than being about learning specific content in order to pass a specific standards-based standardized test, education should focus on developing critical thinking skills. However, current educational reform which relies heavily on standardized testing ignores the effectiveness of such pedagogy, and reinforces the "banking" method that Freire (1970) discussed.

STANDARDIZED TESTING AND NCLB

The notion of a "one-size-fits all" education is at the basis of the standards movement. In the late 1800s, schooling became compulsory for all American children. The goal of this education was the "Americanize" immigrants and to create workers for the burgeoning Industrial Revolution. Scientific measurements were created as a way to improve efficiency in the workplace. In the early part of the twentieth century, educational philosophers were actively examining methodology, strategies, and curriculum.

Standardized testing began during World War I. Coverly and other researchers developed the IQ test, a standardized test which they claimed would sort soldiers who were officer material, that is, more intelligent, from those who were not. Such standardized tests quickly found their way in to the educational system. The social efficiency model was applied to education with the contention that intelligence, as well as "output," what has been learned, could be measured. Curriculum changed to accommodate this measurable output model. Curriculum packages, standardized textbooks, and state and federally mandated standards (Apple, 1995) have been created to feed into this measurable output form of assessment, although studies have shown that this type of education is not effective for all students. Many schools of education advocate problem-based learning, constructivism, and other nonstandardized form of learning and teaching, but more and more legislation is being passed to focus on the "banking" method of standardized curriculum and teaching. Bohn and Sleeter (2000) say that

> the current obsession with standardizing curricula and measuring output will further reduce teacher agency and further marginalize segments of our society that are already seriously cheated by the system. (p. 156)

There is an increased emphasis on "learning the basics" through rote learning, while enrichment education and alternative methodologies are being pushed aside. It is important to also remember that in most schools in the United States, these "transactions" are performed in English.

Current education reform which is based on standardized testing has been adopted by most states, as well as being part of the NCLB. Curriculum standards are being created with formal assessments being linked to these standards. Moreover, the conventional, multiple-choice and short-answer tests that are used almost exclusively test only one type of learning, giving an advantage to one type of learner.

These standards and the assessments are putting "pressure on school districts to standardize and emphasize [certain] content at the expense of

any other concerns" (Bohn & Sleeter, 2000, p. 156). One of the problems
with this standardization is that an assumption is being made "that all students have an equal opportunity to learn" (Bohn & Sleeter, 2000, p. 160).
Such standardization is not taking into account the inequalities that exist
among school facilities, access to materials and resources, and quality of
teachers.

One of the weaknesses of NCLB is that its rigid structure of assessment
and accountability penalizes schools and students that do not conform to
its standards. Schools in areas with low socioeconomic populations are at a
disadvantage, because as research has shown "one of the best predictors,
if not the best predictor, of achievement in a school is the socioeconomic
status of the parents" (Sternberg, 2004, p. 1). Schools with large populations of non-English speaking students are also at a disadvantage with
standards that do not take language differences into account. Children
with special needs are also being measured by the same yardstick that all
other students are.

The stakes are so high for schools that some are resorting to unethical
tactics in order to maintain their position. Cheating by schools, teachers,
and students is not uncommon. For instance, students may be "helped"
on the tests; data may be altered; and scores for traditionally low scoring
students may be excluded. Student drop out rates have increased as
schools either overtly or covertly encourage weak students to drop out
rather than test. "Education becomes increasingly a high stakes game in
which success is defined almost entirely by one's ability to test well enough
through whatever means necessary" (Shapiro, 2000, p. 22).

One issue that is often ignored in the discussion about curricular
reform is that the majority of the teaching force is White. Therefore, even
if teachers are brought into the discussion and decision-making of effective reforms, there is no guarantee that change will be effected that are in
the best interests of all students. A study of educational reform conducted
by Pauline Lipman (Bohn & Sleeter, 2000) in 1998 found that the new system is still based in white privilege. "A predominately white teaching force
is likely to make most decisions through the lenses of white people's experiences and belief systems" (Bohn & Sleeter, 2000, p. 161). This study
points up the urgent need for increased recruitment of teachers of all
races and ethnicities, so that they can not only have a voice and presence
within schools, but also in the state and national decision-making forums.

There is an upside, however, to this concern with standards and standardization. Being explicit about what children need to learn in order to
do well on the tests supports Delpit's (1993) contention that the rules
should be taught to students who do not grow up as part of the dominant
society, that the "cultural capital" be made explicit. "Standards make visi-

ble the expectations for learning that otherwise were implicit" (Bohn & Sleeter, 2000, p. 60).

CONCLUSION

Educational reform is needed in the United States, but the not the type of reform that standardized testing and NCLB support. Rather than instituting reforms that continue to replicate and reproduce the inequities in American society, reform should focus on how schools in the United States can ameliorate the inequalities and inequities in the society. In order to provide equitable education there needs to be political action and educational action; models of education that work for all students; and involvement by all constituents.

The many variables in schools, communities, and students must be taken into account in order for accountability to improve education for all students. Apple (1995) contends that by focusing on the "basic skills," which is what a standardized curriculum and standardized testing does, accountability becomes individualized, which "guarantees its acceptability to a wide array of classes and interest groups" (p. 137). This individualized focus ignores the larger issues that are embedded in American society which impact education. The current educational situation in the United States focuses on individual rights. Therefore, those who have power and money benefit from education while those who do not have to be satisfied with what is left over. This situation creates a disparity and a division by supporting individualism and competition. Apple (1995) asserts that "Alternative pedagogies and curricular models need to be developed in an atmosphere that fosters" (p. 115) improved education for all.

Assessment should be designed with input from all stakeholders so that children's needs are being met equitably. The rigid rules of NCLB leave no room for these variables, and the one-dimensionality of standardized tests do not take individual differences into account. One problem with using standardized tests to the exclusion of any other type of assessment is that they tend to measure superficial knowledge without assessing how one uses the knowledge they have learned. "Achievement is not just about what one knows, but about how one analyzes what one knows, creatively goes beyond what one knows, and applies what one knows in practice" (Sternberg, 2004, p. 4). There are students who do well on these types of tests, and others for whom this type of testing is a poor assessment of their actual learning.

Educational reform should recognize the wide array of learning styles of students, and the variety of content to learn about, and use an array of assessments. "Alternative assessment formats, such as teacher observation, personal communication, and student performances, demonstrations, and portfolios, offer students and teachers a forum where the knowledge or skill to be assessed is grounded in" (Loadman & Thomas, n.d.) and is relevant to life outside the school setting.

Assessment, while the one of the most visible, is only one aspect of what reform should deal with. In order to create more equitable education, more fundamental changes need to be addressed. School, an apparatus of the state, defines what are legitimate knowledge and skills. If, as Freire suggests, the purpose of education is to be liberatory so that a critical consciousness is created in the populace, it then becomes apparent why rigid legislation such as NCLB is supported. The state requires consent of the populace in order to maintain its legitimacy and control. It gains this assent through creating structures which are supported by those in power, and by preventing the development of critical consciousness in the less powerful so that they will not question the status quo.

The No Child Left Behind Act falls short of providing equitable education to all students, because its basic premise is flawed. It relies on the assumption that every individual is alike and should be treated alike. It has mandated initiatives that do not give adequate attention to the issues of a diverse body of learners. Without the involvement of all constituents, the reforms the remediation that many students need will fall short, making NCLB is just one more way in which students from traditionally silenced groups are still keep within a "culture of silence."

REFERENCES

Apple. M. (1995). *Education and power.* New York: Routledge.

Anyon, J. (1980). Social class and the hidden curriculum of work. *Journal of Education, 162,* 67-92.

Bohn, A., & Sleeter, C. (2000). Multicultural education and the standards movement. *Phi Delta Kappan, 82*(2), 156-159.

Delpit, L. (1993). *Other people's children: Cultural conflict in the classroom.* New York: The New Press.

Freire, P. (1970). *Pedagogy of the oppressed.* New York: Continuum.

Loadman, W., & Thomas, A. (n.d.). Standardized test scores and alternative assessments: Different pieces of the same puzzle. *ENC Focus: A Magazine for Classroom Innovators,* 7(2) [online]. Retrieved from http://www.enc.org/focus/assessment/document.shtm?input=FOC-001558-index

Moraes, M. (1996). *Bilingual education: A dialogue with the Bakhtin Circle.* Albany, NY: SUNY Press.

Shapiro, H. S. (2000). The new crisis in education: Who is cheating whom? *Tikkun 15*(5), 21-24.

Sternberg, R. J. (2004). Good intentions, bad results: A dozen reasons why the No Child Left Behind Act is failing our schools. *EdWeek.org* [online]. Retrieved January 24, 2005. http://www.edweek.org/ew/articles/2004/10/27/09sternberg .h24.html

REFLECTION QUESTIONS

1. What are the advantages and disadvantages of curriculum packages?
2. How is power enacted in the classroom and in the educational system of the United States?
3. What is the goal of education?

FOLLOW-UP ACTIVITIES

1. Talk to a school administrator about the standardized tests that her or his school uses? What is the administrator's impression of the accuracy and usefulness of these tests?
2. Talk to a non-English speaker about their experiences taking standardized tests in the US.

FURTHER READING

- Apple, M. (1995). *Education and power* (2nd ed.). New York, NY: Routledge.
- Freire, P. (1970). *Pedagogy of the oppressed*. New York, NY: Continuum Press.

CHAPTER 4

STANDARD AMERICAN ENGLISH

Focus on Profanity as a Social Language Issue in the ESL/EFL Classroom

INTRODUCTION

An increasing number of teachers from the United States are involved in teaching English, either as a foreign language (EFL) in other countries or as a second language (ESL) to students who live within the borders of the United States. Teachers in formal settings, especially public schools and universities, are expected to adhere to certain curricular guidelines, resulting in Standard English being the English that is brought into the classroom. However, whether the English learner is an ESL student in an American classroom, or an EFL student in an international setting, they are exposed to "non-standard" American English through contact with Americans, and through American media and popular culture. Their teacher may even speak a form of "nonstandard" English themselves. With this exposure to various forms of English, these students often perceive that non-standard English and the informal language that Americans use in everyday speech is the "authentic" mode of communication, not the formal English of the traditional ESL/EFL classroom. The desire

ESL, EFL, and Bilingual Education: Exploring Historical, Sociocultural, Linguistic, and Instructional Foundations, pp. 43–52
Copyright © 2010 by Information Age Publishing

43

on the part of young people to communicate "authentically" can present a dilemma to the ESL/EFL teacher. In formal school settings, teachers are expected to adhere to curricular guidelines, which support the teaching of Standard English. What role does social or informal language play? What is the teacher's responsibility to students wanting to learn and use informal English in the ESL/EFL classroom? Where does the teacher draw the line when students want to use the informal English, including profanity, that they have learned from their peers and from American popular culture, English which they perceive as the language that Americans use to communicate in everyday life?

This article examines the issue of social language in the context of students' wanting to learn and use informal English in the ESL/EFL classroom, focusing on profanity. I address these questions using my experiences as an EFL teacher in Poland, as well as from colleagues in various ESL/EFL settings.

STANDARD AMERICAN ENGLISH

Before continuing this examination of standard versus non-standard English, it is important to note that Standard American English is at the center of a heated debate in American education. At issue is whether Standard American English, the English of middle-class White America, is the "correct" form of English, or whether other forms of English, dialects, and language patterns, are equally valid. A number of American educators see this issue not just as an educational issue, but also as an ethical issue. They assert that an insistence on the superiority of Standard American English is an exercise of power by the dominant White culture which devalues minority languages, denying equality and dignity to minority cultures in the United States (Delpit, 1994). If a native speaker of English speaks with a strong accent, or uses a nonstandard dialect, their English is considered substandard, and not worth learning.

I would like to propose that the issue is even broader than the debate within American education. It plays a role in how English is taught to ESL students, as well as whose English is being taught in the EFL classroom. Traditionally, Standard English native-speaker fluency was the goal for all English learners. However, as English evolves and as it spreads around the world, more and more varieties of English are being spoken (Crystal, 2003). There is a movement now to see these variations of English, not as substandard, or wrong, but simply as variations (Cook, 1999), validating different forms of English. This broader view gives the learner more freedom to experience natural language as their learning goal. Although this issue is beyond the scope of this article, this argument has relevance for those teachers who speak a "non-standard" form of English or who are nonnative speakers of English.

ENGLISH TEACHING AND LEARNING GOALS

School systems in the United States offer ESL instruction to students who are nonspeakers of English in order to help them become functional in American society. Internationally schools offer English to students to help them participate in the global marketplace (Phillipson & Skutnabb-Kangas, 1997). Although these reasons are important for students, the goal of English learners of all ages is to communicate and connect with others who speak English. Young people, in particular, want to learn English so that they can communicate with other teens in the language of their music and movie icons. Especially popular are American movies depicting "normal" American life, and American music, such as heavy metal, rap, and hip-hop, which give voice to American youth culture. As English teachers struggle to teach their students formal grammar and pronunciation and the vocabulary that is deemed appropriate and necessary, the students are learning a colloquial, vernacular English that never appears on school examinations. Many teenagers think that the colloquial, and often profane, language that they hear in American popular culture is "Standard" American English.

Slang, including, profanity, is generally not taught in the classroom, partly because it is considered informal language and not appropriate for the classroom setting, but also because slang, in particular, tends to be "changeable according to age, gender, social class, geographic location, time, and so forth" (Charkova, 2007, p. 369). Listening to American popular music, watching movies which depict "normal" American life, and wide-spread access to the Internet have helped students worldwide experience natural English language, which is often informal, full of slang, and can be profane. Many teenagers, in particular, do not make the distinction between what is standard and nonstandard language, and make the assumption that the authentic language they are hearing is "Standard" American English.

The difference between student and educational goals for language learning has become apparent to me over the years that I have taught English in Poland, first as a Peace Corps volunteer in a Polish high school, and later teaching in English summer camps for Polish high school students. When I began teaching in Poland, I taught formal grammar and vocabulary according to the Polish secondary educational curriculum. I discouraged students from using forms, such as "'coz," and "gonna" in their writing, explaining that such informal language was out of place in written communication. Such constructions would not be allowed on a formal standardized examination, so they needed to develop the habit of using formal English in their writing. There were also a few instances when students used profanity, a possibility not covered in nine weeks of Peace Corps teacher training, but such instances were rare, and I addressed the immediate issue and moved on.

Ten years later, at a summer camp for high school students from all over Poland, the issue of nonstandard English, particularly profanity, was more evident. Students frequently used informal English, including profanity inside the classroom, as well as out on the playing field.

Since Poland has undergone major social changes in the past 20 years, I assumed that some of this relaxing of language usage was related to these changes. Young people in Poland are more open than their parents who grew up under Communist rule. However, I also have been around young people enough to know that they like to test the boundaries with informal language, whether their own or one they are learning. Therefore, as I decided to talk to other people who teach in EFL and ESL settings and see what their experiences have been. I did not reach a conclusion about whether this phenomenon is related to social change in Poland, but I learned that it is worldwide.

PROFANITY AS A SOCIAL LANGUAGE ISSUE

As recently as the 1960s and 1970s, it was uncommon to hear profanity on the street, in the schools, and in other public places in the United States. Certain words were banned from the television, and mainstream movies contained very little profanity. However, in the late twentieth century, profanity became more commonplace in everyday American speech, and has become part of the public sphere. When flipping the channels or watching a movie, the viewer can hear a wide range of swear words used by characters of all ages, even young people.

This is not to suggest that profanity among young people is a new phenomenon. Young people have often used this language as a form of rebellion or as a way of asserting their maturity. However, today's young people are surrounded by so much profanity, that it is viewed by them as mainstream language. Hartill (2001) cites a comment by a Boston high school junior who says, " 'To us, it's just the way we talk to each other; it's not offensive' " (p. 21). James Twitchell, an English professor at the University of Florida notes "that kids are not reluctant to swear in public largely because social norms have changed" (Hartill, 2001, p. 21). I believe that this phenomenon is also related to the general relaxing of attention to formal grammar and vocabulary (McWhorter, 2003) redefining what is Standard and nonstandard English.

As a some-time EFL teacher, I am interested in the effects that the public language that students hear has on their perception of English. Of recent interest to me is that this seeming casual use of profanity is beginning to find its way into the ESL/EFL classroom.

When I was first teaching English in Poland, from 1992-1994, I taught at a Liceum, a high school whose students were university bound, in a small town in western Poland. I taught according to the Polish educational curriculum, teaching formal grammar and vocabulary. A few students would occasionally ask me about words or phrases they had heard in a song or a movie, but at that time, their access to American popular culture was still fairly limited. There were also a couple of instances in which students used profanity. This possibility had not been covered in my 9 weeks of Peace Corps teacher training, so I had to rely on my own intuition and initiative about how to best handle these situations. The first instance was when I was demonstrating an idiom, "to chicken out," and was preparing to jump from one table to another. As I climbed on the first table, I told my students what I was planning to do, and one of my students blurted out "Bullshit!" I was so startled, that I started laughing. I then explained that although Paul had used the term correctly, it was an inappropriate word to use in class. Of course, he had heard this in movies and wanted to know why he could not say it, and what he could say instead. I explained that "bull" would be just as effective, and more appropriate. Later, in another class, a student raised his hand, and asked me to clarify something he had heard in a movie. "Do you say 'to hell you say' or 'the hell you say'?" Making one of those thousands of split-second decisions that teachers make everyday, I decided to address the issue, again stressing the appropriateness of when to use such language, then told the class that we would not discuss this topic any more.

In the entire 2 years that I taught at the Liceum, there were only one or two other instances of students using English profanity in the classroom, and I was able to again address the immediate issue and move on. However, the summer of 2003, 10 years later, when I was teaching in an English summer camp in Poland, I was confronted with the pervasiveness of profanity in American popular culture, and had to address this issue repeatedly with Polish students.

I spent July 2003 in a small city in western Poland, teaching at an English immersion summer camp. The camp participants were high school students from all over Poland, who spend 3 weeks taking classes and participating in activities run by American teachers and American young people.

Early in the camp, at an American Field Day event, one student whose team lost a contest, stomped across the field, yelling "f—k, f—k, f—k." I stopped him and told him not to say that. Incidentally, I later heard this same student saying the equivalent word in Polish. I told him that I knew what *that* meant, too, and that I was offended by it, whether in English or in Polish.

In class one morning, students in groups prepared skits to perform in front of the class. Several of the skits contained profanity. I explained each time that although they heard these words in movies and in music, they were not used by all Americans, and that they were not appropriate to use in all situations. Several of the students, male and female, tried to argue with me that they would use the equivalent Polish words in any situation, but I cannot see some of my Polish friends who are teachers allowing students to use such language in their classrooms.

I became interested in this spread of profanity among the students in Poland, so I asked some people who teach in EFL and ESL settings if they have had similar experiences and here is what some of them told me. I found that this desire to use English profanity cuts across genders and all age levels.

Dana (not her real name) who teaches English to retired people in Poland is a recent college graduate. She is 25 years old. Her English is native-like because she spent a number of years in the United States as a child. She takes her role as the teacher of people old enough to be her grandparents very seriously and expects to be treated with equal respect by her students. One man, a retired teacher, who entered the class already knowing some English has been one of her biggest challenges. One of his favorite words is what I will euphemistically refer to as the "F-word." Trying to be respectful of his age and seniority, Dana tried to be gentle in the way she addressed this issue. She told him that it was profanity and should not be used in the classroom. "That is quite a bad word," she told him. The student told her, "You're wrong. Americans say this all the time. It's ok." After several times, she finally decided that his behavior was disrespectful to her and the other students, and just told him, "I don't want to hear it again in my classroom." They had an uneasy truce after that. Finally, he transferred to another class which is taught by a young Canadian woman, and one day she came to Dana and asked, "What should I do about this?" It was the same problem. Having dealt with it in her class, Dana was dismayed that he was treating her colleague the same way. Her first response was, "This is how you say the same thing in Polish. Say to this student, 'K----!' You shouldn't use that word in my class." Of course, she told the young woman that she was just kidding, and told her how she had handled the situation.

Generally, when we think about students using profanity, we think of young people and how they are trying to fit in and how they are testing the limits. I think in a way, even this older man was doing this. As a former teacher himself, I am sure he would not have allowed this kind of behavior in his classroom, and my theory is—some armchair psychology here—that he was trying to establish a power relationship with these young women. Interestingly enough, I met this man on several occasions. I am in a woman in my 50s, and he never used any profanity at all in my presence.

One woman I know told her experiences with teaching adults and university students in Korea. She said:

> I teach at a local university in a suburb of Seoul, Korea. I have witnessed dozens of times, in just one semester, where Korean students swear in English and think it is perfectly acceptable. Korean behavior and etiquette is governed by Confucianism (strict forms of address, respect for elders, knowing your place in society, etc.). If you are older than someone else, he or she will address you formally. If you are younger than someone else, you will be spoken to in an informal manner. All of this leads many Koreans to believe that there is no politeness or respect conveyed in the English language, that it is kind of a free-for-all. It also does not help that many movies and other forms of English-language entertainment are peppered with profanity. My students, before I corrected them, thought it was perfectly okay to say things like "S---!" if they received a paper back with a bad score or I marked them late. Two actually told me that they thought I would be impressed because they were talking like "real Americans."

Here is another example she gave me:

> I used to work at an international company here in Korea. There was a meeting of executives and I was giving a presentation so I was in attendance. One of the Korean managers stood up to introduce himself and said "My name is Mr. Kim. My initials are B.S., so I'm B.S. Kim. You can call me bull--- if you want." He and his Korean coworkers laughed but I cringed and the non-Korean executives looked confused or shocked.

Another woman I am acquainted with teaches middle school students in Korea and she told me:

> My Korean middle school students love English swear words. I let them swear in class as I am happy to get any English production out of them. Occasionally I will correct their use of swear words. They often say "F*ck, shut up." If I am in a benevolent mood I will let them know that it's "shut the f*ck up" and they are really good about correcting themselves after that. When I teach at the public school I try to be more reserved about teaching the students how to use swear words properly, but in a private les-

son or at an academy I am more liberal. I never introduce the words to them, but rather I help them use the words they already know. Also I am from Philly and people use the f-word all the time both in anger and in happiness.

Another woman told me about her experiences in China. She said that her students watched American movies, "which tend to feature a lot of slang/curse words, especially action movies [and] They were absolutely thrilled that they understand at least that part of the movie, if they understood nothing else."

All of these examples have been from EFL classrooms. However, profanity is also an issue in ESL classrooms. An ESL teacher told me that she has heard her high school Spanish students

> use English profanity easily and flippantly, but I don't think they understand the impact made or offense given when spoken to native English students and within that environment. It is the same as when I began learning Spanish. When I heard a swear word spoken in Spanish (before I knew what it was) it sounded beautiful; however, I cringed when I found out what it meant. Still, when I would say the word to myself (I don't use profanity or encourage it), it didn't have the same impact as hearing it in English ... I think it is the same for students. Their native language profanity seems to be much more impactful than speaking it in English.... A strong profane word in one language may translate with not as much profane quality in another language.

This teacher also said:

> Because students do encounter it in movies or books, I will appropriately express the meaning to them, but I do it in an educational manner. Some of my other students would be insulted or embarrassed if I encouraged or allowed profanity to flow freely in my classroom.

Another ESL teacher told me that he has found that his middle school aged boys like to try out profanity, more than girls do. He said that the boys feel like it is an expression of their toughness and helps them fit in with their peers.

I did ask one of my ESL colleagues who had also taught in EFL settings if she thought students used profanity more in ESL or EFL settings. She offered this opinion: when learners "are using an L2 outside of their cultural homebase" they may not be as quick to use profanity. It may partly be that "in another country [they] may be acting on their best behavior or may have taken cultural cues from listening to their classmates and how they speak." Imitating American culture in their country is one thing, but in the United States where they are the "outsider" is another. I looked for some research to support this notion one way or the other and could not find any studies that had been done on the use of profanity by English learners except for the one by Charkova (2007) which indicates that this area is understudied.

CONCLUSION

As I write this, I am thinking about my own reactions to the language the Polish students were using. I would be lying if I said I never use informal English, including profanity. I do. Still, I believe that it has no place in an EFL classroom, and will continue to tell my students that despite what they hear, not all Americans approve of cursing as a form of regular communication (Dolliver, 2002).

However, to return to the broader issue of Standard English, beyond the issue of profanity, I wonder what are the motives for and consequences of imparting to them my White American middle class values of "correct" language? Is the insistence that they learn formal grammar and pronunciation, and the vocabulary that is deemed appropriate and necessary, rather than the colloquial, vernacular English that never appears on any school examination, denying them ability to communicate effectively in English with all native speakers? More importantly, is this insistence on the use of Standard American English, the English of my White middle class American culture, presenting English learners with too narrow a view of what it means to be an American? Is it teaching the students to devalue the equality and dignity of minority cultures in the United States, and around the world?

REFERENCES

Charkova, K. D. (2007). A language without borders: English slang and Bulgarian learners of English. *Language Learning, 57*(3), 369-416.

Cook, V. (1999). Going beyond the native speaker in language teaching. *TESOL Quarterly, 33*(2), 194-195.

Crystal, D. (2003). *English as a global language* (2nd ed.). Cambridge, England: Cambridge University Press.

Delpit, L. (1994). *Other people's children: Cultural conflict in the classroom*. New York: The New Press.

Dolliver, M. (2002). Wash your mouth out. *Adweek, 43*(3), 26.

Hartill, L. (2001). Would you please not repeat that? *Christian Science Monitor, 93*(74), p. 21.

McWhorter, J. (2003). *Doing our own thing: The degradation of language and music and why we should, like, care*. New York: Gotham.

Phillipson, R. & Skutnabb-Kangas, T. (1997) Linguistic human rights and English in Europe. *World Englishes, 16*(1),27-43.

REFLECTION QUESTIONS

1. How are slang and profanity social language issues?
2. What are the ethnical implications for an insistence on Standard English?
3. What is a teacher's responsibility in teaching and upholding Standard English?

FOLLOW-UP ACTIVITIES

1. Ask a teacher how he/she handles these issues in his/her classroom.
2. Research where the rules for Standard American English come from.

FURTHER READING

- "Do you speak American" at http://www.pbs.org/speak/seatosea/standardamerican/
- McWhorter, J. (2003). *Doing our own thing: The degradation of language and music and why we should, like, care*. New York, NY: Gotham.

PART II

Linguistic and Sociocultural Issues in ESL/EFL Education

OVERVIEW

"We know what we are, but know not what we may be."

—William Shakespeare

Whether we are talking about an international university student, a child in an elementary ESL class, or the parent of a student who is an English language learner and has special needs, we have to be aware that the person is more than a language learner. The person who comes into this situation has a background and experiences that have shaped their identity, who they are, and how they communicate and interact with other people.

Their socialization may have taught them social and cultural norms that are different from those they are experiencing living in another place. They have moved from being like those around them to being a "stranger." In his work, sociologist Bauman (2001) suggests that membership in a group provides at least a perception of comfort and security to those within the group, giving a sense of order and a sense of belonging

ESL, EFL, and Bilingual Education: Exploring Historical, Sociocultural, Linguistic, and Instructional Foundations, pp. 53–55
Copyright © 2010 by Information Age Publishing
53

for those who are included. Those who do not fit the pattern become the "other" or "stranger."

There are multiple definitions of stranger, but the general perception is that a stranger is someone who is not of one's group. Gudykunst and Kim (2003) state that "anytime we communicate with people who are different and unknown and those people are in an environment unfamiliar to them, we are communicating with strangers" (p. 19). Therefore, there are degrees to which someone can be a stranger, and how this will affect communication and interaction with others.

When we are communicating and interacting with someone whose background is very similar to ours we can read their communication cues and are generally comfortable following their lead, with an easy give and take of ideas which is largely unconscious. However, when communicating with a stranger, no matter the distance, anxiety and insecurity about the communication can quickly arise, and can further inhibit communication. For effective communication to take place, adjustments, based on what the participants are learning about each other's communication styles or patterns, must be made to improve transmission of messages to be better understood, or to use a different frame of reference for interpreting the messages.

Teachers often comment that certain groups of students, especially if they are in the minority in a school, tend to hang out together and sit together in the cafeteria. If we think about our perceptions of group membership, this is neither unusual nor is it surprising. We all find ourselves gravitating toward someone we perceive is more like us when we are in a strange or stressful situation. By understanding how identity influences communication and interaction within groups and among different groups, an educator can help students bridge these gaps by creating a space where the various groups can get to know one another, and become more comfortable communicating together.

Educators may find themselves in the situation where they need to serve as advocates not only for their students but for the parents and families of these students who may not speak English well and may not understand the social and cultural norms of the American educational system. This set of essays focuses on social and cultural issues that interact with linguistic issues for the bilingual/ESL learner and educator.

- Chapter 5: "That Is a Bank? When Knowing English Isn't Enough" examines the importance of social and cultural knowledge in language learning.
- Chapter 6: "Language Learning and Intercultural Competence: Negotiating Polish-American Identity" provides an analysis of case studies of two Polish-American female college students.

- Chapter 7: "The Path to College Graduation: Providing Support for Middle School Students Who Are Hispanic" examines data from research conducted on how middle school students who are Hispanic perceive college and how to prepare for the career of their choice. (I would like to acknowledge the assistance of Dr. Laura McQueen and Luz Rodriguez in the preparation of this material, and thank the Program on Ethnicity, Culture, and Health Outcomes for their generous support.)
- Chapter 8: "Not Ready to Sit and Knit: A Look at Aging and Learning English" focuses on issues related to learning English when the learner is an older adult.

REFERENCES

Bauman, Z. (2001). *Community: Seeking safety in an insecure world.* Cambridge, England: Polity Press.

Gudykunst, W. B., & Kim, Y. Y. (2003). *Communicating with strangers: An approach to intercultural communication* (4th ed.). Boston, MA: McGraw-Hill.

CHAPTER 5

THAT IS A BANK?

When Knowing English Isn't Enough

When international university students arrive in the United States for the first time, they experience a variety of feelings which may be unrelated to their ability to use English. After all, most of them have achieved a high enough degree of proficiency in English to have been accepted by the university. However, because communication takes place within a social and cultural environment, knowing the language is not always enough. Communication with others and understanding the new environment is influenced by cultural, sociocultural, psychocultural, and environmental factors, our own and others', which serve as filters influencing the interpretations we make of the new environment and those around us (Gudykunst & Kim, 2003). Therefore, international students, their teachers, and their mentors should be aware of some of the specific issues international students may face and how to address these issues to ensure that the students have an academically and socially successful sojourn in the United States. Research has shown that the unique challenges that international students have in American universities can be ameliorated with support.

ESL, EFL, and Bilingual Education: Exploring Historical, Sociocultural, Linguistic, and Instructional Foundations, pp. 57–68
Copyright © 2010 by Information Age Publishing

THREE MAIN AREAS FOR SUCCESS
AMONG INTERNATIONAL STUDENTS

International students in the United States, whether they are native English-speakers or English Speakers of Other Languages (ESOL), face unique challenges when attending American universities. According to research (Al-Sharideh & Goe, 1998; Boyer & Sedlacek, 1988, Furnham & Alibhai, 1985; Olaniran, 1996; Selvadurai, 1992; Soter, 1992; Zhao, Kuh, Carini, 2005), the three main areas that are important to support for success among these students are: community building and social activities; personal coping skills; and academic assistance, such as tutoring, and study skills, as well as knowledge and information about the academic programs. Each of these areas can provide support in their personal and academic lives.

The information in this chapter is based on research studies as well as conversations with international students about some of the surprises they found when they arrived in the United States or at their university. As well as focusing on some information about American life, in general, and about academic programs, specifically, that may present challenges to international students in the United States, I offer suggestions on helping international students adapt to life at an American university.

LIFE IN THE UNITED STATES

For most students their adjustment to life in the United States begins the minute they step off the plane, because the involves their first direct interactions in American society. Unless the student is being met and escorted to their residence, they will immediately have to begin coping with making purchases, such as a bus or train ticket, or taking a taxi to their destination.

One man told me he was shocked when he landed in the United States and he had to pay for a luggage cart at the airport. He said luckily he had some American money with him. Although many concessions use credit cards, it is a good idea to advise students to arrive in the United States with a little cash, an assortment of bills, not just $100 bills. Some dollar bills are good to have on hand.

International students may not be aware of sales tax, and that the price advertised is usually without sales tax. One day as I was waiting for my bus at the airport I saw two young Polish girls run into this problem. They wanted to buy some chips and did not understand why the sales clerk was asking for more money than was shown on the sign. Therefore, teaching students that most American states charge sales tax on items sold in stores, and that this sales tax is a percentage that is added to the total of your purchase is important.

Students should also be informed that the rules about and the amounts of sales tax vary from state to state. One of the problems of trying to describe anything about the United States is that while there are federal laws, each state has its own rules and legislation, too, so that what is true in one state may not be the same in another state. Sales tax is one of these things. In some states, you pay a sales tax on everything you buy in a store. In other states, you do not pay sales tax on food. In other states, there is no sales tax. Therefore, students need to understand that if an item is priced $4.99, there is a good chance that this item could really cost around $5.30.

Most international students will need to open a bank account when they settle in to university life because it makes their financial life go more smoothly. There may some confusion about types of accounts offered and what the students financial needs are. However, even the physical structure of the bank can surprise students. A few years ago an English teacher from Shenyang, China came to study for a master's degree in secondary education at our university. When she arrived I took her to a small branch bank near the university so that she could open a checking account. This bank is a small square one story building. Later the student told me that she was very surprised that this was a bank. She was from a large city in China and to her a bank is a large multistory office building.

Across the street from this bank is a church. While there are not churches on every corner in the United States, there are many churches and other religious buildings, such as synagogues, temples, and mosques. Students planning to study in the United States should to try to understand this facet of American culture. Many people in the United States belong to some kind of religious organization, and many Americans profess to be members of a religious group. Because freedom of religion is seen as part of the country's heritage, many people view the ability to practice their religion as one of their most important rights. Some Americans assume that others also affiliate with some type of religion, and may ask questions that the international student may find intrusive. It is also not unusual for American Christians to invite others to attend their church. Sometimes the object is proselytizing, but more often the object is a way of inviting the person to be part of their social group.

Another issue that may come up is housing. Some international students are accustomed to living in closer quarters than most Americans. Americans live in apartments and houses just like people in all countries. However, Americans tend to live in larger spaces than many international students are accustomed to. A couple and their children may live in a three-bedroom house, or it may be the home of only one or two people. It is unusual for more than one family to live in a house or an apartment. Some cities even have ordinances about the number of people who can live in a dwelling. International students are often not aware of such laws and may find themselves in a living situation that is illegal.

The Chinese student I mentioned earlier also told me that she was struck by the differences in the American and Chinese approaches to food. She found Americans to be quite wasteful with food, something she was not accustomed to. However, she was more struck by the differences in how food is presented. She compared a restaurant in China which has a name like Good Home Cooking with dishes such as Snow Upon the Mountain (tomatoes sprinkled with sugar) to the Grab 'N Go on campus with its Big Gulp (a very large soft drink).

One final aspect of American life that is important for international students to learn about is that most Americans also own and drive a car. Unfortunately, in many towns and cities in the United States, there is not a good public transportation system, and many places are not well-designed for people who are walking. It is possible for international students to get a driver's license, but they will need someone who can help them learn to drive, as well as help them figure out how to buy a car, car insurance, and so on.

There are many other issues that may come up in daily life for the international student, but these are one that international students have specifically mentioned to me. Tipping in restaurants, how to behave as a guest in someone's home, telephone etiquette, and many more everyday issues can present challenges for the international student.

ACADEMIC LIFE

The university student who arrives on an American campus already has a lifetime of educational experiences to build their perceptions and expectations on. However, like any other aspect of life in another culture education has its own set of cultural and societal norms and rules.

First of all, it is important to clarify how Americans in the United States refer to postsecondary education. In many countries, the term "college" has a specific meaning and "university" has another meaning. While there are differences in the United States between colleges and universities, generally, in everyday speech, people use the words interchangeably. For example, someone may ask "Where did you go to college?" One can answer that question by saying "I went to Sawyer College," a small private school which has one year technical programs, such as auto mechanics or massage therapy, or you could say "I went to college at Purdue," even though Purdue is a major research-one university. In this way, college is used to mean any postsecondary education.

The American degree-granting system may also be different from what the international student is accustomed to. Most American universities and colleges offer 4-year degrees, a BA, bachelor of arts, which is usually a degree in the humanities or social sciences or similar fields, or a BS, a bachelor of science, a degree in science or mathematics and similar fields. There are some colleges which offer 1- or 2-year technical degrees or associate's degrees; however, the first academic degree that most people receive is a 4-year degree.

The next level of degree is the master's degree. Again it can be an MA or an MS depending on the field. It is usually takes 18 months to 2 years to complete a master's degree. The student usually takes 11-16 courses, depending on the program. Usually the student also has to write a master's thesis or complete a master's project.

The PhD, or other doctoral degree, is the highest level of degree awarded. How long it takes to complete and the requirements vary from degree to degree. The PhD is considered a terminal degree and generally there is not a degree rank beyond that, as opposed to some systems in other countries which grant postdoctoral degrees based on professional and academic rank.

Generally, no matter what the major, the student eventually develops a plan of study. This plan helps the student decide when and in what order to take courses. Unlike some university systems, the American university system requires that students take core courses, general college courses, such as English, math, and science courses, before embarking on their major course of study.

Classes in American universities are designated by the number of contact hours and credit hours they have. Contact hours are how many hours a week a course meets. The credit hours has some relationship to the number of contact hours, but it is not always a one-to-one relationship. A 3-hour credit course, which is the norm, is a class that usually meets 3 hours a week. Science classes, for example, are often four credit hours—3 hours for class and 1 hour for lab. However, a class in which a student is expected to observe at a school for 40 hours during the semester, may also be a 1-hour credit course.

Class schedules vary from course to course and university to university, but a three-credit hour course may have one of several configurations. Usually classes that meet during the day meet for a 50-minute period three times a week—Monday, Wednesday, and Friday, or for 1 hour and 20 minutes twice a week, Monday/Wednesday or Tuesday/Thursday. Evening classes usually meet once a week for about 2 hours and 45 minutes. The international student may have to learn to recognize these configurations if they are different from what he/she is accustomed in his/her home educational environment.

Many American universities are on the semester system. A semester is either 15 weeks plus 1 week for exams or 16 weeks plus 1 week for exams. As with everything else about higher education in the United States, it depends. Most American universities begin their fall semester around the end of August or beginning of September. Some universities have a short fall break, usually 1 or 2 days. They also have a break at Thanksgiving—the fourth Thursday in November. The final week of classes is usually the first or second week in December, with the exam week(s) following. After a 3-4 week break, the spring semester begins. It may start the second or third week in January and goes until the first or second week in May, again with a week or two for exams. There is always a week-long spring break around midsemester.

For the international student who comes from a country like Poland, these dates may feel odd. In Poland, for example, what they call the winter semester begins in October and goes until mid-December when they take a break. They return in January to finish classes and exams, then take a 3-4 week winter break. Classes resume in late February for what they call the summer semester. The summer semester lasts until mid to late June. Unlike in the United States, summer school offerings are not the norm. In the United States, most universities offer summer school classes. The schedules have many variations with the classes generally meeting more frequently, and the semester being shorter during the regular academic year.

Besides scheduling and such institutional issues, the international student may have other challenges in trying to adjust to academic life in the United States. At the beginning of one semester a Chinese graduate student asked me how he could find out what books he should buy for his courses and other information about his classes. I told him several times that he would find this information on the course syllabus. He finally smiled, and asked me, "What is a syllabus?" I was so surprised, that I never asked him if he did not understand the word or if he didn't understand the concept. To explain, I gave him the syllabus for my class, and we looked at the different parts of it, so he would understand how to read one. Although every instructor makes their course syllabus a different way, they generally have the same type of information: information about the course; how to contact the instructor; what materials are needed for the course; what assignments there are; and the course schedule.

Office hours, set times when instructors are usually available for students to consult about the class, are generally listed on the syllabus. With the widespread use of e-mail, many instructors prefer that students send an e-mail to ask questions that are easy to answer, such as, When is the exam? How many points is the quiz? Instructors may have posted office hours, usually hours that they are available for consultation with students before and after class.

During office hours and appointments, instructors usually expect the meeting with the student to last 15-30 minutes. Instructors often will talk to students who drop-in. However, because the instructor usually has set this time aside for other work, the student should be prepared not to talk very long. If what the student needs to talk about may take more than 15 minutes, the student should schedule an appointment. Sometimes, international students do not understand these boundaries. They assume that if the professor has an open-door policy, it is always open for them for as long as they want to talk. On the other hand, if they are not accustomed to office hours, or to instructors who offer assistance to their students, they may not realize what the purpose of office hours are.

Although there are numerous other issues that may impact an international student's success at an academic university, the final point I would like to focus on is one that is often misunderstood by international students. It is very important that they understand what is meant by academic integrity because students can fail assignments, fail courses, and even be expelled from the university for breaking these rules.

All universities have an *academic integrity policy* which explains the way that that institution interprets academic honesty and integrity. Each university has individual policies, but there are some universals, such as cheating on work and examinations for the class; lying to an instructor; and plagiarism, the unauthorized use of other's intellectual property.

Cheating includes copying another student's work, or allowing another student to copy your work. Cheating on exams is another issue. In some courses, the instructor expects students to do all their work individually. However, sometimes students are allowed and even encouraged to work with other students. The international student may not understand when sharing work is acceptable, and when it is not. Therefore, it is best for the instructor to make these policies clear, and for the international student to check with the instructor if unsure.

Plagiarism is a serious offense in American universities. Any time a student writes a paper for a class they need to be sure they know what constitutes plagiarism and what citation style the instructor expects. If they are not familiar with doing citations, most universities have a writing lab or perhaps someone at the library who can help the student with this.

BUILDING SUPPORT SYSTEMS

There must be systems in place on university campuses to ensure the academic success, retention, and eventual graduation of international students. Research shows that students who successfully meet the challenges of their first year are more likely to continue their education and will graduate. Other research shows that the unique challenges that international students have in American universities can be ameliorated with support programs. Studies show that the three main areas that are important for success among these students are: community building and social activities; personal coping skills; and academic assistance. The roles of "classroom advocate," "cultural advocate," "language advocate," and "academic advocate," which Christison and Stoller (1997) identify as ways in which universities can support language minority students, are connected to these areas.

On campuses where there is a university-level intensive English program (IEP) program, the administrator of these programs serve as advocates for their programs and their students, and by default, they often become advocates for other language minority students on campus. The language program administrator is often called on to help smooth over language and cultural differences that may arise between language minority students and other people and entities on the campus, serving as an advocate for the students as well as a liaison with the institution.

Community Building and Social Activities

Community building and social activities can help international students more easily overcome some of the stress and anxiety (Olaniran, 1996; Selvadurai, 1992) that "they face in adapting to a foreign living and learning environment" (Zhao et al, 2005, p. 209) and can help them develop adequate personal coping skills. Several studies (Al-Sharideh & Goe, 1998; Furnham & Alibhai, 1985) have shown that students who have strong friendship and social support networks, especially with American students, tend to adapt more quickly and easily.

A peer-mentoring program is one proven support system. Peer-mentors who are American students as well as other international students would give language minority students a learning community and support group that extends beyond the classroom. Although culture shock is inevitable, such support can help these students more easily understand and overcome adjustment problems.

Christison and Stoller (1997) point out that two common areas of concern for international students are the school environment, and adjustment to the community. A well-established mentoring network would help the students cope with some of these issues more easily. For example, a mentor can help smooth some of the confusion surrounding the different routines in the new school environment by explaining about exam schedules or helping understand a syllabus. A good mentoring program could also help with community adjustment by helping students adapt to daily routines, showing them how and where to take public transportation, and so on.

Personal Coping Skills

These community building and social activities are also important for helping students develop personal coping skills. Not only could it provide information about how to contact counseling and other services available on campus and in the community, a mentoring program could provide support for students in personal coping by organizing activities in which both mentors and mentees can participate.

International students also may have some unique needs based on sociocultural variables, and differences in educational styles and expectations. These programs, and IEP administrators, can serve as "cultural advocates" for international students by alerting counseling and other such services on campus of potential problems that may arise and giving advice about how to be culturally sensitive to these issues.

Academic Assistance

The final area which research identifies as important for success with international students is providing various levels and types of academic assistance. Academic assistance may be developing academic English language skills (Krashen, 1982; Thomas & Collier, 1997, Zamel, 2004), as well as skills and knowledge about the American system of education (Soter, 1992).

A support program could serve as a "classroom advocate" (Christison & Stoller, 1997) for international students by helping students and teachers identify areas of possible misunderstanding. It may be necessary to provide examples of misunderstandings, such as difference in eye contact between American culture and other cultures, or whether copying is plagiarism or deferring to an expert.

Support services can also serve as "cultural advocates" (Christison& Stoller, 1997) in the academic arena by helping students and teachers understand that there are cultural differences in educational styles and objectives. For example, a student may not believe that it is acceptable to ask questions of the teacher, while an American teacher expects students to ask questions for more information and clarification. Helping both recognize and understand these differences can help avoid breakdowns.

Oftentimes mainstream educators become frustrated with an international student's language skills without realizing that the problem may be more complex than language issues. Many educators do not realize the difficulty of learning English at a sufficient level for academic purposes and that international students may have different background knowledge than American students. An intermediary who can serve as a "language advocate" is an important role. A few approaches include: pointing out to faculty that the amount of reading and writing is often difficult for a non-native speaker; international students often lack adequate study skills; they may have trouble comprehending new material that is presented orally without reading it; and they may not feel capable of participating spontaneously in class (Christison & Stoller, 1997).

Finally, the role of "academic advocate" is important to help students understand how to be successful and to help faculty understand how their non-native speaker students can "meet the conceptual and linguistic demands of their courses" (Christison & Stoller, 1997, p. 151). She suggests that there be support to help the student develop a plan for overcoming the problem, such as suggesting that the student: ask if they can tape-record lectures; prepare for class by completing all readings; find a dependable study partner; sit near the front; and ask for clarification.

Christison and Stoller (1997) also states that suggestions to faculty can focus on classroom strategies, and creating a positive affect. Some suggestions are: being aware of body language; write key phrases and all homework assignments legibly on the board; encourage students to ask questions; learn students' names; and focus on delivery. She also suggests that providing a checklist to faculty can be useful. Workshops and brown bags can also be effective ways of spreading the word.

CONCLUSION

At a meeting in preparation for a faculty trip to Taiwan, one of the Taiwanese faculty spoke to us about some Taiwanese customs, especially regarding eating. She told us not to stand our chopsticks up in our rice bowl and to not hold our rice bowl in both hands, like a beggar would. These things sounded funny to us, but they are just the type of cultural and social information that it is important for a newcomer to a country to understand, especially one who is going to live for a time in the country. Many cultural and social differences may have nothing to do with language; therefore, even if an international student speaks perfect English, and even if he or she has a flawless American accent, there will be times when knowing the language just is not enough.

REFERENCES

Al-Sharideh, K. A., & Goe, W. R. (1998). Ethnic communities within the university: An examination of factors influencing the personal adjustment of international students. *Research in Higher Education, 39*, 699-725.

Boyer, S., & Sedlacek, W. (1988). Noncognitive predictors of academic success for international students: A longitudinal study. *Journal of College Student Development, 29*, 218-223.

Christison, M., & Stoller, F. L. (Eds.). (1997). *A handbook for language program administrators*. Burligame, CA: Alta Book Center.

Furnham, A., & Alibhai, N. (1985). The friendship networks of foreign students: A replication and extension of the functional model. *International Journal of Psychology, 20*(6), 709-722.

Gudykunst, W. B., & Kim, Y. Y. (2003). *Communicating with strangers: An approach to intercultural communication* (4th ed.). Boston, MA: McGraw-Hill.

Krashen, S. (1982). *Principles and practice in second language acquisition*. Oxford, England: Pergamon Press.

Olaniran, B. A. (1996). Social skills acquisition: A closer look at foreign students on college campuses and factor influencing their level of social difficulty in social situations. *Communication Studies, 47*, 72-88.

Selvadurai, R. (1992). Problems faced by international students in American colleges and universities. *Community Review, 12*(1-2), 27-32.

Soter, A. (1992). Whose shared assumptions? Making the implicit explicit. In D. Murray (Ed.), *Diversity as resource: Redefining cultural literacy* (pp. 30-55). Alexandria, VA: TESOL.

Thomas, W. P., & Collier, V. (1997, December). School effectiveness for language minority students. *National Clearinghouse for Bilingual Education Resource Collection Series, 9*. Washington, DC: National Clearinghouse for Bilingual Education.

Zamel, V. (2004). Strangers in academia: The experiences of faculty and ESOL students across the curriculum. In V. Zamel & R. Spack (Eds.), *Crossing the curriculum: Multilingual learners in college classrooms* (pp. 3-17). Mahwah, NJ: Erlbaum.

Zhao, C. M., Kuh, G. D., & Carini, R. M. (2005). A comparison of international student and American student engagement in effective educational practices. *Journal of Higher Education, 76*(2), 209-233.

REFLECTION QUESTIONS

1. How can university students (American and international) help one another have successful and positive experiences in American universities?

2. How can you prepare international students to cope with these and other types of social and cultural issues they may experience on American campuses?

3. What are some characteristics of effective mentoring programs for international students?

FOLLOW-UP ACTIVITIES

1. If you are an American student, interview an international student about their experiences in the university setting and compare them to yours.
2. If you are an international student, interview an American student about their experiences as a university student and compare them to yours.

FURTHER READING

- Gudykunst, W. B., & Kim, Y. Y. (2003). *Communicating with strangers: An approach to intercultural communication* (4th ed.). Boston, MA: McGraw-Hill.
- Spielberg, S. (Director). (2004). *The terminal*. [Motion picture]. United States: Dreamworks.

CHAPTER 6

LANGUAGE LEARNING AND INTERCULTURAL COMPETENCE

Negotiating Polish-American Identity

INTRODUCTION

In *Modernity and Ambivalence*, Zygmunt Bauman (1991) asserts that modernity abhors ambivalence. The modern world seeks to classify and bring order to everything, including people. Modern nations can tolerate those who are outside their definition of who belongs, because these outsiders can, at least, be classified, often in terms of ethnicity. However, "strangers," as he calls them, people who are not so easily classified, people who do not neatly fit the description of insider or outsider, are treated with suspicion, and even hostility, because of their ambiguity. However, Bauman (1991) goes on to say that the person who can successfully integrate their own identity so that they can bridge the two worlds becomes a "universal stranger," one who "is 'fully at home' only with himself [*sic*]" (p. 95).

While Bauman (1991) situates his notions of "stranger" and ambiguous identity at the national level, they are useful in examining identity issues

ESL, EFL, and Bilingual Education: Exploring Historical, Sociocultural, Linguistic, and Instructional Foundations, pp. 69–82

at the individual level. This notion of "stranger" is evident in the experiences of two young women of Polish ethnicity who grew up in the United States, and who identify strongly with one national identity while living in another. These two young women were participants in a research project focusing on language and cultural identity. Although both of them identified themselves as "Polish," the researcher identifies them as "Polish-American," not so much as an ethnicity, but as individuals who have integrated two cultural identities into their individual identities. Bauman's (1991) description of the "stranger" demonstrates how others see these individuals, not so much as how the individuals see themselves. Their status as "stranger" is supported by his notion of people who do not neatly fit the description of insider or outsider, whose identities are ambiguous. However, their stories demonstrate that, while it is not necessarily easy, it is possible to be "competent" in more than one culture, and to be comfortable with more than one cultural identity.

The purpose of this chapter is to examine the experiences of two young women and how they each negotiate the ambiguities and complexities of their identity. I will first consider the notions of national identity and ethnic identity formation, and the effects that such a collective identity can have on an individual. Then I will present some of the characteristics of Polish ethnic identity. Next I will examine how the people in her life were instrumental in creating a Polish identity for each young woman. Finally, I will discuss how being Polish-American has created an ambiguous identity for them, so that they are a stranger no matter where they are.

IDENTITY FORMATION AND BEING A STRANGER

If one visualizes identity as a web, it is easy to see how the various strands that make up the individual's identity are interconnected and interdependent. Most of the strands of identity are created by how that person makes meaning of her life and the world around her, through her interactions with others. The strongest and most dominant strands are those that connect the individual to the larger world, creating "collective identity." The strands of collective identity, the part of an individual's makeup that shows the person as "an extension of the collective ... a distinguishable part of the whole" (Casey, 1996, p. 221), are created by the individual's interactions with family, friends, peers, teachers, television, books, culture, political conditions, anything in the world around her. There are also contradictory elements within the collective identity, which provide the tension that gives shape to the web of identity.

Identity formation theory is one way in which the modern world seeks to categorize people. Erikson's (1963, 1968) work on identity formation examines stages of development, beginning with a lack of awareness of identity, then progressing to a stage or stages where identity is being examined, even questioned, which is often called an identity crisis. The final stage of identity development is gaining a sense of identity. According to Erikson (1968), "ego identity formation is particularly critical in young adulthood, specifically during the college years, because the extent to which the identity issue is resolved determines the success or failure of adult development" (as cited in St. Louis & Liem, 2005, p. 228). Erikson's stages of development have been used as the basis of some models of ethnic identity formation. These models, supported by existing research in the field (Arce, 1981; Aries & Moorehead, 1989; Phinney, 1991, 1992; Phinney & Tarver, 1988; Spencer & Markstrom-Adams, 1990; Streitmatter, 1988), support the notion that "the formation of a positive sense of ethnic identity is considered to be essential to the successful development and adaptation of ethnic minority youth in American society" (St. Louis & Liem, 2005, p. 230). The social aspects of ethnic identity formation theory (Tajfel, 1978) make it is a useful construct for an examination of Bauman's notion of the "stranger."

The scientific principles of the modern world seek to order and classify everything. These principles indicate that for a nation to be properly classed as such, it should have a homogeneous, that is, easily classified, population. Although the nation may be comprised of one or more ethnic groups, national identity is an attempt to unify a population legally, linguistically, culturally, and ideologically. The creation of a national identity is an attempt to establish a shared history and a common culture so that the population has a "shared feeling of belonging together ... being different from all others" (Steiner, 1995, p. 307). This construction of a "collective consciousness" around economic, political, and geographical conditions creates boundaries which define a nation's citizenry, and does not allow or encourage deviation. By constructing these boundaries, this one "way of being" is legitimized, creating inequalities for those who do not conform to what becomes "the values of the dominant elite" (Bauman, 1991, p. 107). Bauman (1991) says that these boundaries must "be both exclusive and comprehensive [so that] nothing left inside may be irrelevant to the total design" (p. 24). This kind of social engineering gives a sense of order and a sense of belonging for those who are included, but those who do not fit the pattern become the "other." Native members of a community learn knowledge and attitudes about what is relevant and taken for granted in the community, so that they feel both security and assurance about their shared worldview within the community. National identity gives the individual the opportunity to develop a sense of belonging to something larger than herself. However, when national identity is essentialized so that there is only one "right" way of being an American or a Pole, the individual has little opportunity to develop and express a unique sense of self within this nationalistic context.

Bauman (1991) recognizes that the "other" can consist of those who are totally outside the boundaries, but more often in a nation there are those he calls "strangers" whose identity is ambiguous, defying classification. They occupy an area of uncertainty between the "in" and "out," with characteristics of the "in," but cannot really be classified as "in" or only with uncertainty. The stranger who assimilates never really becomes part of the dominant culture because she never gains full acceptance by the dominant culture. The native does not believe "that the stranger will [ever] become like the native and will never see the world though native eyes" (Bauman, 1991, p. 84).

Bauman (1991) asserts that nations are formed as an attempt to "eliminate the strangers" (p. 63). The nation extends the rights and privileges of citizenry to those it deems desirable, those it can classify. Assimilation of the stranger is usually the goal, or she may be stigmatized as "other, or "untouchable." The stranger may be banished completely or placed outside the realm of normal social contact, as in a ghetto.

An individual, even though he or she tries to assimilate, may not be at home anywhere. He or she becomes a "universal stranger" who "is 'fully at home' only with himself [sic]" (Bauman, 1991, p. 95). This comes only with incredible effort and the ability to create a self-identity that is integrated and the ambivalence is integrated. The uncertainty of where one belongs can create feelings of loneliness and isolation in one who assimilates. Jacob Wasserman (1991) explains that

> it is characteristic of individuals crossing the margin between social groups that they are not only uncertain about their belonging to the group they are ready to enter, but also about their belonging to the group they are leaving. (as cited in Bauman, 1991, p. 118)

POLISH NATIONAL IDENTITY

To better understand the issues faced by the young women in this study, it will be helpful to examine the history of the country to which they give part of their allegiance, and from which their ethnic identity has its roots. A brief overview of Polish history will establish this context.

The history of Poland as a nation began in the tenth century when Mieszko I, founder of the Piast dynasty, became king of the group of West Slavic people inhabiting an area in Central Europe. In 966, he decreed that the people of Poland become Roman Catholics. Over the past 1,000 years, the borders of Poland have shifted and altered with changing political conditions in Europe, but the identity of those people who call themselves "Polish" has remained defined by their Slavic ancestry, the Polish language, Roman Catholicism, and the many customs and traditions of their culture. According to Davies (1984) the Polish language "is the essential ingredient of Polish nationality" (p. 330). Volenski and Grzymala-Moszczynska (1997) assert that being Roman Catholic is such a part of the Polish identity that church membership is seen by many as not just a religious duty, but as a patriotic duty.

In the mid-1500s, Poland, the largest state in Europe, was home to a diverse group of people. There were numerous languages, ethnic groups, and faiths represented in the country, although the Polish language became the language of government, commerce, science, and culture. This diversity promoted tolerance and "encouraged a strong tradition of education" (Davies, 1984, p. 317) as the various groups shared with and inspired one another. Despite this atmosphere of tolerance, the Poles "had a reputation for exaggerated pride in their country [believing] that traditional Polish ways were superior to those of all other nations" (Davies, 1984, p. 269). This was partly based on the desire of the Polish aristocracy to assert that their roots were not the same as the common people's.

In the 1700s, Poland lost much of its territory, and finally ceased to exist as a political entity. Its territory was partitioned among Germany, Austria, and Russia. Although Polish systems of education, government, military, and so forth were abolished under the Partitions, "many of the more intangible elements of old Polish life—their culture, languages, religions, social and political attitudes" (Davies, 1984, p. 316) survived. The suppression of their national rites and rituals resulted in a Polish patriotism which "became the object of an intense, secret, and highly developed mysticism" (Davies, 1984, p. 270). This "underground religion" of Polish patriotism was modeled after the Catholic Church, and those who followed it believed that it was something worth dying for. According to Davies (1984), the literature that period, the Romantic Period, was a driving force in keeping this desire for freedom alive and representing it as a spiritual journey.

By the end of the nineteenth century, partitioned Poland was laying the groundwork for reunification. Many Poles rejected the notion of Pan-Slavism which came into vogue during the 1800s. They were afraid of being submerged in Russia's history. They developed their own Piast Concept (based on the Piast Kings) of a Poland that was made up of Polish-speaking people; that was totally Catholic; and that was resistant to Germany. This established the Polish language and Catholicism as integral parts of the Polish national identity. The link with the Catholic Church was strengthened at the beginning of the twentieth century as the Polish clergy struggled together with the Polish people to create a cohesive nation. However, there was not total unity, and friction continued to exist between the political and church arenas, even after Poland regained its independence after World War I, until the horrors of World War II brought about a "the undivided Catholicity of the Polish nation" (Davies, 1984, p. 342). After World War II, Poland's boundaries changed again and its population became fairly homogeneous, because the reformation of the state had changed borders and had relocated people from other ethnic and national groups. The Communists under the Soviet regime adopted the Piast Concept, because it represented the Poles as not just Russian puppets, but a separate people with their "distinct ethnic composition and its own national territory" (Davies, 1984, p. 326).

Poles define their national identity primarily by language and religion. Polish nationals feel a responsibility and moral duty to one another, and Poles extend this no matter where they live. According to Bauman (1991), the "anticipation of enmity is indispensable in the construction of enemies" (p. 54). History has taught the Poles to anticipate enmity from those who not speak their language or practice Polish Catholicism. Many Poles who immigrate to other countries carry this wariness with them.

TWO YOUNG WOMEN

At first glance, these two young women, Anna and Beata, seem to be very much alike. They are both ethnically Polish, and self-identify as Polish. Their parents moved to the northeastern United States from Poland and have encouraged their daughters not to lose their Polish roots. They are both students in prestigious American colleges, and they look and act like "average" White, middle-class American college students. They speak English with the fluency of native speakers, although they both speak Polish at home with their families. Both young women emphasized their parents' role in creating their Polish identity, although for Anna it was more an instilling of pride of heritage, while for Beata it was a reminder to not forget her roots. However, there is one major difference in these women's lives that has made their experiences very different. Anna grew up in a fairly tight-knit Polish community that kept and shared many traditions from their homeland. Beata, on the other hand, did not. Her family was just one of a few Polish families in the small northeastern town where they settled.

Anna's Background

Anna, a sophomore at an Ivy League university, was amazed when she learned that she was the first Polish person that many of her college friends had ever met. Even though she was born, and has always lived, in the United States, she has always been surrounded by Polish people, Polish food, Polish customs, and the Polish language. Her parents, who immigrated to the United States as young people, met, married, and reared their children in a community in the Northeast that has many inhabitants who immigrated from Poland. There are several Polish Catholic churches, and numerous Polish delis and groceries in the community. Because of her experiences growing up in such a community, Anna told me she identifies herself as Polish more readily than as an American, and has great pride in her Polish heritage, which was instilled by her parents. Anna's parents came to the United States as young adults. Because of her parents' example, Anna sees Poles as being very hard-working and "dedicated to success." Neither of them knew English when they arrived and were able to overcome language barriers enough to succeed and be happy in their new lives. However, they have maintained strong connections to the Polish language, as well as Polish customs and traditions.

> Being Polish, for me, is a source of great pride ... I probably got this pride, so much pride, because my parents are always reminding you, "You're Polish." ... We have Polish stuff going on around our house. Polish TV is on Sundays and we watch Polish TV. Polish radio is all day Sunday in our area ... My dad listens mostly to Polish music ... My mom gets Polish magazines and stuff. Almost all their friends are Polish. We go to a Polish church. The area that we live in, there's just a lot of Polish people there.

Anna stressed the importance of the Catholic Church as a religious and social center to the Polish culture and to herself. Until she left home and went to college, Anna was unaware that there were differences in Catholic traditions.

> A lot of our ... Polish traditions revolve around Catholic holidays. So, our Christmas is a little bit different and our Easter is a little bit different from Americans', and even our house will have a few symbols that are a little bit different, like maybe you've seen ... like a K + M + B written over it (the door). They are the initials of the three Kings that came to Jesus and you just write that.... Our church even hands out chalk that has been blessed.... A lot of our traditions and stuff, I thought it was a Catholic thing to do, all Catholics did it, and I met all these other Catholics, [who said] "I've never heard of that." And they are very faithful Catholics so, maybe it's a Polish Catholic tradition.

Beata's Background

Beata's experience living the United States was different than Anna's. Beata, a senior at a small, private liberal arts college, was born in Lublin, Poland. She and her parents moved to rural Maine when she was 8 years old. She attended kindergarten and first grade in Poland, and when she arrived in the United States with her family, she was placed in second grade, even though she knew no English. Although they have lived in the United States for 15 years, Beata said that her parents have never really adjusted to life here. They plan to return to Poland with Beata when she graduates from college.

Although Beata's parents reminded her constantly of her Polish roots, it did not create the same sense of pride for her that it did for Anna. They did not live in a large Polish community, and this insistence on their Polish heritage created a sense of isolation for her.

> My parents were always holding on so tightly to their Polish roots ... I felt that that caused me even more isolation because I was always told that I'm different ... you know, you're not part of this. Not, not that it was bad. It just wasn't our[s] ... It's foreign. They really didn't want to assimilate at all ... my parents still don't feel like they belong here. That's largely why they want to get back to Poland, because it's something that is really hard when you don't have your roots established here to actually become part of this.

Although Beata's parents were Catholic, they did not have a tradition of church involvement such as Anna's family had. She became involved in Intervarsity Christian Fellowship when she was in college and says that her connection with this group helped her to not only learn about religion, but also helped her learn more about herself. This connection was a turning point for her. She felt isolated and rebellious up to this point in her life, because she was unsure of her identity and felt like her parents were trying to force one identity on her, while her life in the United States tempted her with assimilation.

> Trying to assimilate as much as I possibly could to this culture. I never really valued what I had either, as far as my roots went. When I left my parents to go to college, I didn't have that pressure of Poland, Poland, Poland, all the time on me. And I was left alone for those 4 years pretty much to figure out who I was and now that I'm leaving, I can accept the Polish part of me, because I know who I am, but that's not what defines me, if that makes sense. For a long time I tried to be so American, but that didn't really satisfy me. I was always, "Who am I? What's going on?" I hated it. I hated myself. And, then, I didn't want to be Polish because Poland was way over there and what did that mean to me, you know ... And I think, throughout all of it, I think that they [her parents] were kinda wondering who I would become.

Language Issues

Language became a symbol of the differences between Beata and her parents. She feels that her parents' lack of English contributed to her feelings of isolation. When they lived in Poland, she had done well in school and her mother had been active in her schooling.

> I learned the language quickly, but I knew, ... even though I had good grades still, I was always a little behind, as far as the language aspect was concerned ... when you compare me to other kids. And I think that caused me to withdraw a lot socially, you know, because I couldn't really communicate that well and, whereas in Poland, I ... had a lot of friends ... my mom was wanting to hang out the other moms and I think that has a lot to do to bring the kids together. Whereas here, my mom didn't speak English really that well ... it was harder for her and my dad to learn it, so she never really attended the ... parent meetings, so she didn't really know anybody. So that isolated me, I think.

She became fluent in English by the time she was in the seventh grade. With fluency in English came feeling more a part of the American culture, and fitting in with her American peers.

Anna's experiences with language were rather different. Before Anna started school, she and her twin sister always conversed with their parents in Polish, although they were learning to understand English by watching television. After starting school, Anna and her sister responded increasingly in English, even though their parents continued speaking to them in Polish. Speaking in Polish was reserved for those times when they played "grown-up"—when they imagined stepping out into the public sphere as adults.

> My twin sister and I would, we would play grown-up. You know ... put on high heels and carry a purse ... pretend they are playing grown-ups. Well Maria and I thought that playing grown-up meant like my mom and all her friends, and they all spoke Polish, so when we played grown-ups, we had to speak in Polish. And we'd be Basia and Krysia, which are our middle names, which are very Polish-sounding. When we played Basia and Krysia, we had to talk in Polish, because that's what grown-ups did.

Because such bilingualism is common in Anna's community, she had never examined its implications for her private life, until she went to visit family in Poland and realized that Polish was not only the "grown up" language, but also the "children's language." Anna thinks that her perception of Polish as "the other language" has created a barrier in her relationships with her parents. She knows that she and her parents literally do not understand one another sometimes.

Polish was always the other language for me ... the language of the grown-ups. Last year when I came to Poland, and I'm looking at all my little cousins talking to their parents in Polish, and ... it's the children's language, also. I was, like, "It's not like the 'other' language." Kids in Poland understand their parents, and I felt a little jealous ... it kind of hit me, I can never really understand my parents and they can never really understand me, because we don't speak the same language. It's very evident when I get angry at my parents, and I'm trying to express something that I'm angry about, I just switch to Polish because it's just the most annoying thing in the world to try to yell at them, or make a point, and them be like, "I don't even know what is that. What do you mean?" It's very frustrating to have that barrier. So I'll just switch to Polish, because I don't even want to deal with it. But it's kind of sad, that I will never understand them, completely, even though I understand a lot, I don't know everything, and they don't understand everything. I know every kid's like "You don't understand" about their parents, but I think it's a little bit more evident for me.

DISCUSSION

Although both of these young women identify themselves as Polish, they are embedded in American culture and society and have learned to fit into the culture of White America. Both look and dress like "average" middle class, White college students. American television programs were their early English teachers, and television and school provided them with an entrée into American culture and society. They both learned to communicate well enough that their written and oral English skills are like those of a native English speaker. They both sound like average White, middle class American college students, both their accents, and their use of current American idiom. Their experiences illustrate ways in which Erikson's stages of identity development play out.

As they are entering adulthood, both young women are learning to examine and articulate their experiences as children who grew up in two cultures. As a child, Beata had a greater struggle than Anna, because she did not grow up in a community in which she felt she really belonged. Beata was the one who was "different" in her classes and in her community. She had to cope with the tensions created by the difference between the expectations of American society and the expectations of her parents. Her "identity crisis" came at an early age as she was confronted with the ways in which who she was at home did not fit with the ways she was expected to be in the community and society. However, as young adult, she feels that she has resolved many of the issues that created such uncertainty in her life and she thinks she is able to balance her Polish and American sides.

Although Beata struggled with her identity throughout middle school and high school, going to college and being separated from her parents helped to finally see herself more clearly. As a young adult she was able to, as Erikson (1968) suggests, resolve some of the issues that were creating a feeling of isolation and confusion for her. She feels that she has resolved her identity as someone who is Polish and American. She realizes and is reconciled to the fact that she will never really fit into either world, that she will always be a "stranger." However, her parents are planning to back to Poland when she graduates from college and to take her with them. How strongly her sense of self is established may be tested in this new environment. She may again experience an "identity crisis" as she tried to fit into this new world. However, if she truly has resolved her issues, she may have created a self which is a "universal stranger," one who is able to live comfortably with the ambiguity of her identity.

Anna, on the other hand, grew up in a community where she did not experience being different. She was unaware of her identity. She did not have the childhood struggles that Beata had, but she is now being confronted with the realization that she does not feel like an American, despite being born in the United States, being an American citizen, and having always been surrounded by American cultural values. Her first language is not English. Her religion is not the Protestantism that pervades American society. Her home community honors another nation and culture. "Being Polish" is a big part of who she is, and Anna does not want to give it up. However, in spite of her identification as a Pole, when Anna enters the public sphere in Poland, she experiences a shift. She does not have all the knowledge and attitudes that are taken for granted in the Polish sphere. She speaks Polish well, but misses some of the nuances natural to a native speaker. She does not have all the knowledge and attitudes that are taken for granted in the Polish sphere, so experiences ambiguity there as well.

Now, as a young adult, Anna has stepped out into the larger society of the United States, out of the safety of her community, and for the first time is experiencing herself as the "stranger." Until she went to college, she was surrounded by people and traditions that defined her as "in." As a young adult she is leaving her home community, and Anna is beginning to experience a sense of being "other," realizing that she does not fit exactly into the larger American or Polish communities. In her young adulthood, she is experiencing an "identity crisis." She has become aware that her identity is out of step with what she thought was her identity. As her experiences with her parents and in Poland demonstrate, she is not as Polish as she always thought she was. Now she is realizing that although she is "in" in her community, she does not fit exactly into the larger American or Polish societies. This ambiguity is what makes her, by Bauman's (1991) definition, a stranger.

Because of her circumstances, Anna lives in more of a state of ambiguity than Beata. If Anna is a "native" anywhere, it is in the Polish-American community in which she grew up. It created a public sphere for her that overlaps with her private sphere. This assimilated community is where she knows what is relevant and taken for granted in the community, where she feels secure about a shared world-view with the community. However, this community exists within the larger public sphere of the United States. Anna has always been surrounded by American culture and American values, through television and school, especially. However, she does not feel like an American. Because her upbringing was so entrenched in Polish culture and traditions, she is often not aware of what American traditions are. She belongs to a community that rejects many American traits and embraces those of another nation and culture.

At age 19, Anna is just beginning to realize that she is a stranger in two worlds. Until she went to college, she had not been confronted with the ways in which she was in her home community did not necessarily conform with the ways of the larger culture society in which she lives. She is the daughter of Polish parents who have instilled a pride of Poland and of being Polish in her, even though she was born and has lived her whole life in the United States. She grew up in a community that reinforced this pride. She feels strongly that people should honor the traditions of their home culture and plans to raise her children to speak Polish and to carry on Polish traditions. She feels that "being Polish" is a big part of who she is and she does not want to give it up. To Anna, being Polish consists of two important elements—language and religion.

This ambivalence can create problems of alienation and isolation for Anna, or she can learn to use it to create herself as a "universal stranger," one who is able to live comfortably with the ambiguity of her identity. According to Phinney (1993), the individual who successfully accepts and internalizes their ethnic identity will have a better sense of well-being and satisfaction in their lives. This resolution is not an easy task and will require some hard decisions on her part. She will have to give up parts of herself and accept other parts that do not fit both societies. She may have to develop a chameleon-like changeability, so that she can fit more easily into the society where she is at the moment. She may even find that she needs to be more one way than another. Now that she has experienced her "otherness," she will never be able to go back to the comfortable life that she had before she left home, even if she returns to her community. However she decides to deal with her ambiguity, whether she rejects it or integrates it, she will have to accept that she is always and everywhere a stranger.

REFERENCES

Arce, C. (1981). A reconsideration of Chicano culture and identity. *Daedalus, 110*(2), 177-192.

Aries, E., & Moorehead, K. (1989). The importance of ethnicity in the development of identity Black adolescents. *Psychological Reports, 65*(1), 75-82.

Bauman, Z. (1991). *Modernity and ambivalence*. Ithaca, NY: Cornell University Press.

Casey, K. (1996). The new narrative research in education. *Review of Research in Education, 21*(1), 211-253.

Davies, N. (1984). *Heart of Europe: A short history of Poland*. Oxford, England: Oxford University Press.

Erikson, E. (1963). *Childhood and society* (2nd ed.) New York: Norton.

Erikson, E. (1968). *Identity: Youth and crisis*. New York: Norton.

Phinney, J. (1991). Ethnic identity and self-esteem: A review and integration. *Hispanic Journal of Behavioral Sciences, 13* (2), 193-208.

Phinney, J. (1992). The multigroup ethnic identity measure: A new scale for use with diverse groups. *Journal of Adolescent Research, 7*(2), 156-176.

Phinney, J. (1993). A three-stage model of ethnic identity development in adolescence. In M. E. Bernal & G. P. Knight (Eds.), *Ethnic identity: Formation and transmission among Hispanics and other minorities* (pp. 61-79). Albany, NY: State University of New York Press.

Phinney, J., & Tarver, S. (1988). Ethnic identity search and commitment in Black and White eighth-graders. *Journal of Early Adolescence, 8*(3), 265-277.

Spencer, M. & Markstrom-Adams, C. (1990). Identity processes among racial and ethnic minority children in America. *Child Development, 61* (2), 290-310.

St. Louis, G. R., & Liem, J. H. (2005). Ego identity, ethnic identity, and the psychological well-being of ethnic minority and majority college students. *Identity: An International Journal of Theory and Research, 5*(3), 227-246.

Steiner, J. (1995). *European democracies* (3rd ed.). New York: Longman.

Streitmatter, J. L. (1988). Ethnicity as a mediating variable of early adolescent identity development. *Journal of Adolescence, 11*(4), 335-346.

Tajfel, H. (1978). *The social psychology of minorities*. New York, NY: Minority Rights Group.

Volenski, L. T., & Grzymala-Moszczynska, H. (1997). Religious pluralism in Poland. *America, 176*(6), 21-23.

REFLECTION QUESTIONS

1. How relevant is Bauman's notion of the universal stranger to the lives of immigrants/?

2. How do Anna's and Beata's educational experiences reflect those of students who are not children of immigrants?

3.   What are other characteristics, besides language and religion, that might impact immigrants from other countries or cultures?

FOLLOW-UP ACTIVITIES

1.   Interview someone who immigrated to the United States as a small child and compare their experiences to those of Anna and Beata.
2.   Compare immigration patterns of different groups to the United States. Which groups maintained their community and identity more strongly than others? Why?

FURTHER READING

- Hoffman, E. (1990). *Lost in translation: A life in a new language.* New York, NY: Penguin.
- Kaplan, A. (1994). *French lessons: A memoir.* Chicago, IL: University of Chicago Press.

CHAPTER 7

THE PATH TO COLLEGE GRADUATION

Providing Support for Middle School Students Who Are Hispanic

Although the population of Hispanics is rising rapidly in the United States, the numbers of Hispanic students who complete high school and graduate from college is disproportionately low. Besides issues which historically have created barriers to education for minority groups, such as poverty and language issues, many of these students are classified as "first generation college goers," a group that traditionally has difficulty attaining college graduation. Interventions intended for the first generation college student that are designed for the specific needs of the Hispanic population can give these students needed assistance to successfully attend and graduate from college.

The literature on the academic success of Hispanic students (Espinoza-Herold, 2003; Jones & Fuller, 2003) shows that the drop-out rate for this group is higher than for any other group, and that college matriculation is disproportionately low for this population. According to the U.S. Census Bureau (2003) reports, among 16-19-year-old Hispanic students there were approximately 530,000 high school dropouts in 2000, a dropout rate of 21.1% for this specific population. (Hispanic will be used throughout

ESL, EFL, and Bilingual Education: Exploring Historical, Sociocultural, Linguistic, and Instructional Foundations, pp. 83–92
Copyright © 2010 by Information Age Publishing

this essay to conform to the term that the U.S. government uses to identify this population.) "The Latino youth dropout rate was more than three times greater than the 2000 non-Hispanic 'white alone' dropout rate of 6.9 percent" (Fry, 2004, para. 3). With such high drop-out rates it is not surprising that the percentage of Hispanic students who actually attend college is low. According to data collected in fall 2005 (Knapp, Kelly-Reid, Whitmore, & Miller, 2007), 3.9% of college students enrolled in 4-year degree programs are Hispanic, a number that can be directly related to the high dropout rate among Hispanic high school students.

FIRST GENERATION COLLEGE STUDENTS

There are a number of factors that contribute to the high drop-out rate and low college attendance for Hispanic students (Espinoza-Herold, 2003; Jones & Fuller, 2003; Nieto, 2005; Ogbu, 1992; Ogbu & Simons, 1998). Racial, ethnic, cultural, socioeconomic, and linguistic biases combine to create a school climate that leads to academic disengagement of many minority students. High school Hispanic students become increasingly disengaged from school resulting in their drop-out rate being the highest among all groups (Espinoza-Herold, 2003).

One factor that comes into play is college-attendance by parents. According to a literature review by Tym, McMillion, Barone, and Webster (2004) on first generation college students, 40% of college freshman who are Hispanic attending 4-year colleges are first generation college goers, compared to 20% of White students. A study by Striplin (1999) indicated that first generation college students also struggle with "doubts about their academic and motivational abilities; they may think they are not college material" (Tym et al., 2004, p. 5). Since many Hispanic students tend to be underprepared academically for college, have low SAT/ACT scores, and often require remediation in English and mathematics (Schmidt, 2003), these doubts can be based in the reality of their lack of academic preparation for college.

Tym et al. (2004) also found that although the "families of first-generation students sometimes discourage them from going to college [leading] to alienation from family support" (Tym et al., 2004, p. 2), this does not seem to be the case for Hispanic families. "Family surveys conducted by the Education Department show that more than 9 out of 10 Hispanic parents expect their children to attend college—a figure in line with results for both black and white parents (Tym et al., 2004, p. 5). According to Schmidt (2003), Tomas Arciniega, who is the president of California State University at Bakersfield which has a Hispanic student population of about 36%, agrees that Hispanic students have support from their parents. However, Arciniega believes that they lack appropriate knowledge about how to negotiate the system.

PURPOSE OF THE STUDY

The purpose of this study was twofold: one objective was to determine if middle students who were Hispanic were interested in nursing as a career; the other objective was to determine if they wanted to go to college and what they knew about the college admissions process. An earlier case study by McQueen and Zimmerman (2006), a nursing educator, and a multicultural education specialist, formed the basis for this project. In the earlier case study, a Hispanic nurse reported on how she perceived her college experience. She answered questions which addressed the concerns and perspectives of the two disciplines represented, education and nursing. The participant connected her nursing school experience to her family; being a minority, particularly Hispanic; and her own sense of self. The respondent stated that Hispanic students will have a better chance of success if they form connections, and receive peer, faculty, staff, and family support during their college experience. For the purposes of the current study, the research design focused on two points addressed by the participant:

- The recruitment of Hispanic students should begin as early as freshman year of high school.
- Many high school Hispanic students perceive limited opportunities for higher education and for financial aid to pay for it, therefore needing better information from high school educators and college recruiters.

Therefore, this project was designed to determine if middle school Hispanic students see college an option, and what their perceptions of college and careers are. The data can be used to determine how to set up early interventions for these students.

This project was partially supported by a grant from the Program on Ethnicity, Culture, and Health Outcomes which focuses on issues related to racial or ethnic healthcare disparities. Quality care to underserved populations can be obtained through putting in place successful measures for the recruitment and retention of members of target minority populations. Since the Hispanic population is generally underrepresented in nursing, the data from this project can be useful in developing a plan for addressing low college admissions rates in general, as well as this disparity in the healthcare workforce.

In this phase of the project a needs analysis survey for middle school Hispanic students in Guilford County and Forsyth County in North Carolina was developed, tested, and implemented. This sample data was used to explore Hispanic children's interest in attending college and their possible interest in nursing as a career.

METHOD

This project, which was designed according to Institutional Review Board (IRB) guidelines, relied on survey methodology to gather information. One questionnaire collected demographics and information on middle school students' interest in nursing as a career. A needs assessment questionnaire collected data to assess how the children perceive their educational needs. The questionnaire asked questions about their future career plans, their knowledge about nursing as a career, and general knowledge about college to determine what kinds of information the target group, middle school Hispanic students, may need to help them choose among career options. The final questionnaire asked for their perceptions of personal characteristics closely associated with those who are nurses.

A descriptive research approach was used to associate and summarize the needs assessment and additional findings that arose out of the project. Frequency counts and correlations examined the relationships among variables, specifically with data from those students who indicated they had considered nursing as a career.

Participants

When this project was originally designed, the plan was to recruit participants from middle schools in Guilford County, NC. School population data was gathered and schools were selected which had the largest population of Hispanic students. A practicing nurse who is Hispanic was recruited to assist with the project. She translated the questionnaires into Spanish and was prepared to interpret as needed. Due to school board rules and requirements about conducting research with students, gaining access to the schools posed a problem time-wise. Another concern was that parents would not return consent forms in a timely manner, a common issue in research with children. In a strategy session, the nurse suggested that there may be more reliable access to participants if they were to go to churches where Hispanics attended. She arranged this, contacting Catholic and Protestant churches in Guilford County and neighboring Forsythe County. Several of the Protestant churches agreed to allow the research team to come after services and recruit participants. This approach proved successful. The surveyors were able to explain directly to the parents what the research project was about, gain their consent immediately, and implement the questionnaires.

Hispanic children, ranging from the study's target ages of 10-14 completed the questionnaires. Of 58 respondents, 28 were female, and 30 were male. The students recruited to participate in this project reported attending third to ninth grades (see Table 7.1). The data collectors also observed interactions between parents and children which provided further data about the children's knowledge about educational and career options.

Survey Instruments

Three survey instruments, written in English and Spanish, containing a combination of scaled responses and narrative responses were developed for this project. One questionnaire collected demographic information. A second questionnaire asked questions about student perceptions of career options, including nursing. The participants then responded to a questionnaire of characteristics of an effective nurse.

After the students completed the questionnaires, the data were analyzed according to the type of data collected. Quantitative data was entered into an Access database, then transferred to Statistical Package for the Social Sciences (SPSS) 14. Frequency charts and cross-tabulations of selected variables were analyzed for relationships.

Table 7.1.   Frequency by Grade, Gender, and School District

Grade	Male	Female	Guilford County	Forsyth County
Not reported	0	1	1	0
3	0	2	0	2
4	3	3	4	2
5	8	5	6	7
6	8	4	5	7
7	9	7	6	10
8	1	5	5	1
9	1	1	2	0
Total (N = 58)	30	28	29	29

Table 7.2.   Frequency of Parental College Attendance

n = 15	*Father Attended*	*Mother Attended*
Respondent wants to attend college (*n* = 14)	6	14
Respondent may want to attend college (*n* = 1)		1
Respondent wants to attend college—reported by siblings (*n* = 6)	2	3

RESULTS

This project addresses the hypothesis: Hispanic students do not see nursing as a career choice, because they do not see college as an option because they lack information on how to prepare for college/university admission. This chapter will focus on the second part of this hypothesis: the students' desire to go to college and their knowledge about the process. The two variables that this chapter will focus on are represented by the following questions from the questionnaire:

- What do you plan to do after high school graduation?
- Has anyone in your family gone to college?

Of the 58 respondents, 48 of them said that they definitely wanted to go to college after high school graduation. An additional 7 of the respondents indicated that they were not sure, but might want to go to college after high school.

The respondents also indicated who in their family had gone to college. There were 58 respondents, some of whom were siblings, resulting in a total of 90 parents. Of the 58 respondents, 15 indicated that their father and/or mother had gone to college. Of these 15, there were 3 sets of siblings; therefore the actual number of parents who attended college was 12 (see Table 7.2). Of the total sample, 13.3% of the parents of the respondents reported having attended college.

DISCUSSION

When looking at these data in light of aspirations for education, they support Tym et al.'s (2004) findings that Hispanic students do want to attend college and that their parents expect them to do so, and contradict other findings (Striplin,1999; Tym et al., 2004) that indicate that students from this population have lower educational expectations. As is found in research about attainment of college by parents (Hahs-Vaughn, 2004; Tym et al., 2004), all of the students who had a parent who attended college, indicated that they would attend college.

Although the middle school students in this study reported that by and large they are interested in attending college, research on Hispanic students show that actual college admissions and retention is quite low (Espinoza-Herold, 2003; Fry, 2004; Jones & Fuller, 2003; U.S. Census Bureau, 2003). Based on the results of this study and the earlier case study (McQueen & Zimmerman, 2006), it is evident that further research needs to be done to determine why many Hispanic students do not go on the college. One avenue for further investigation would be to determine what changes once these students reach college-age. Do they still want to go to college? What barriers prevent them from going?

Considering the data gathered from this study and the previous case study, one barrier that seems to exist for these students is lack of appropriate information and guidance about attending college. A study by Hahs-Vaughn (2004) comparing first-generation college students and non-first-generation college students found that familial support is a strong factor in how well a student succeeds in college. However, even if the family is supportive, studies (Tym et al., 2004) of students who are first generation college goers points toward the importance of interventions to help these students succeed.

> Students whose parents did not attend college are more likely than their non first-generation counterparts to be less academically prepared for college, to have less knowledge of how to apply for college and for financial assistance, and to have more difficulty in acclimating themselves to college once they enroll. (Tym et al., 2004, p. 1)

This population of students also has a lower retention rate, pointing to the need for mentoring, academic, and social support within the college environment and the "social capital" gained by participation in nonacademic experiences for first generation students may be a way that these students can acquire the "cultural capital" that helps them succeed in college (Pascaralla & Terenzini, 1983, p. 278). Social and cultural capital refers to knowledge and values that one has from being part of a cultural or social group, the rules by which one becomes and stays a member of the group (McCollum, 1999). In the educational setting, "students with social and linguistic competence matching the requirements of the curriculum are advantaged over ... students who possess different cultural and linguistic knowledge" (McCollum, 1999, Discussion section, para. 4).

Gullatt and Jan (2003) propose that there are three types of programs that help provide precollege students with the necessary academic and social capital they need to successfully be admitted and complete college. Informational outreach programs focus on providing information and guidance about college, but provide "little or no academic intervention in the way of actual instruction" (Tym et al., 2004, p. 17). Career-based outreach programs provide services to help students identify career options and how to translate these into college degrees. Academic support programs provide actual "instructional services designed to increase student performance in college preparation classes or to improve students' opportunities to enroll in such classes (Gullatt & Jan, 2003)" (Tym et al., 2004, p. 17).

CONCLUSION

According to Gullatt and Jan (2003), students need a combination of appropriate academic preparation and they need to develop social capital, underlying knowledge about attending and being successful in college that will help them develop the belief that they can succeed. One possible solution to the problem of lack of knowledge about college admissions would be to develop community information sessions in which parents and children are given information about college admissions, such as high school coursework needed, how to score well on SATs/ACTs, and how to apply for financial aid.

Based on data from this study and the previous case study (McQueen & Zimmerman, 2006), it is reasonable that a community informational outreach program should be developed which addresses the specific needs of Hispanic students. The purpose of the program would be to provide college information and career information. It would also meet the needs of the community by involving families. Materials would be prepared and presented in English and in Spanish to reach the widest group possible. The program could be offered in various centers which are frequented by the local Hispanic population, such as churches, community centers, and outreach programs in the community. Career specialists would inform parents and children about careers and how to prepare for them. Educational specialists would inform parents and the children about college admission requirements, financial requirements, financial aid opportunities, and retention requirements, and other preparations for college. Using a community outreach approach which focuses on educational and career information will enable the parents and children to see the relationship between career choice and educational opportunities.

Education is more than teaching students facts and figures in the confines of a classroom. Education must go beyond the traditional classroom and beyond the standard curriculum to provide students, and their families, with the knowledge they need for having educational options and career choices that fulfill their dreams.

REFERENCES

Espinoza-Herold, M. (2003). *Issues in Latino education: Race, school, culture and the politics of academic success*. Boston, MA: Allyn & Bacon.

Fry, R. (2004). High school dropout rates for Latino youth. Retrieved from (http://www.ericdigests.org/2004-3/latino.html

Gullatt, Y., & Jan, W. (2003). *How do pre-collegiate academic outreach programs impact college-going among underrepresented students?* Washington, DC: Pathways to College Network Clearinghouse.

Hahs-Waughan, D. (2004). The impact of parents' education level on college students: An analysis using the beginning postsecondary students longitudinal study 1990-92/94. *Journal of College Student Development*. Retrieved from http://findarticles.com/p/articles/mi_qa3752/is_200409/ai_n9455916/pg_9

Jones, T., & Fuller, M. (2003). *Teaching Hispanic children*. Boston, MA: Pearson Education.

Knapp, L. G., Kelly-Reid, J. E., Whitmore, R. W., & Miller, E. S. (2007). *Enrollment in postsecondary institutions, fall 2005; Graduation rates, 1999 and 2002 cohorts; and financial statistics, fiscal year 2005*. Retrieved from http://nces.ed.gov/pubs2007/2007154.pdf

McCollum, P. (1999). Learning to value English: Cultural capital in a two-way bilingual program. *Bilingual Research Journal, 23*(2&3), 113-134.

McQueen, L., & Zimmerman, L. (2006). Using interpretive narrative research methodology in interdisciplinary research projects: Issues in the education of Hispanic nurses. *Journal of Nursing Education, 45*(11), 475-478.

Nieto, S. (2005). *Affirming diversity: The sociopolitical context of multicultural education* (4th ed.). Boston, MA: Allyn & Bacon.

Ogbu, J. (1992). Understanding cultural differences and school learning. *Education Libraries, 16*(3), 7-11.

Ogbu, J., & Simons, H. (1998). Voluntary and involuntary minorities: A cultural-ecological theory of school performance with some implications for education. *Anthropology & Education Quarterly, 29*(2), 155-188.

Pascarella, E. T., & Terenzini, P. T. (1983). Predicting volunteer freshman year persistence/withdrawal behavior in a research university: A path analysis validation of Tinto's model. *Journal of Educational Psychology, 75*(2), 215-226.

Schmidt, P. (2003, November 28). Academe's Hispanic future: The nation's largest minority group faces big obstacles in higher education, and colleges struggle to find the right ways to help. *The Chronicle of Higher Education, 50*(14): A8. Retrieved from http://chronicle.com

Striplin, J. J. (1999). *Facilitating transfer for first-generation community college students*. *ERIC Digest*, ED430627.

Tym, C., McMillion, R., Barone, S., & Webster, J. (2004). First-generation college students: A literature review. Retrieved from http://www.tgslc.org/pdf/first_generation.pdf

U.S. Census Bureau. (2003). *School enrollment: 2000* (C2KBR-26). Washington, DC: Author.

REFLECTION QUESTIONS

1. What can educators do to improve the retention rate of Hispanic students, at any age?
2. How effective is mentoring in helping student decide on career paths and in helping them stay in school?
3. What other groups of students might be favorably impacted by early intervention programs?

FOLLOW-UP ACTIVITIES

1. Interview a high school career counselor about how they guide students toward careers.
2. Investigate what types of outreach programs there are in your community for students who are considered at-risk.

FURTHER READING

- Gutierrez, J. (2006). *We won't back down: Severita Lara's rise from student leader to mayor.* Houston, TX: Piñata Books.
- Smith, L. (2005). *What every high school student doesn't know … yet: A guide for the college-bound.* Boulder, CO: Blue Mountain Arts.

CHAPTER 8

NOT READY TO SIT AND KNIT

A Look at Aging and Learning English

Generally, when one thinks of an aging population, one thinks of the problems they face: health and healthcare issues, decreased involvement in community and social life, lack of access to resources. Old age is also traditionally seen as a time of slowing down, of taking a less active role in society, a time to relax, and enjoying one's grandchildren. The problems that the elderly face, and the expectations for their lifestyle are reality.

However, an alternative reality is developing among many aging citizens. Even though they may be retired from active work life, many are not ready to just "sit and knit" as one Polish woman told me. Many have access to disposable income; many are in good health; many are well-educated; many are still mentally active. They are not ready to take on the traditional role of the elderly who sit by the fireside.

A review of research literature shows that few studies have been conducted on foreign language learning in this population. In particular, the topic of second language acquisition in older learners of English does not seem to have been systematically studied in the field of Teaching English to Speakers of Other Languages (TESOL). However, there are some relevant studies about aging and learning from outside of the field of education and second language learning, such as sociology, psychology, neurobiology, gerontology, and speech and hearing that offer some useful

ESL, EFL, and Bilingual Education: Exploring Historical, Sociocultural, Linguistic, and Instructional Foundations, pp. 93–104
Copyright © 2010 by Information Age Publishing

background information for examining this issue. A comparison of some of this research shows that there is interconnectedness among these areas which impacts language learning as a person ages. Being aware of these issues can help the language educator design a program and use strategies that take advantage of an older learner's strengths while structuring learning in a way to minimize their weaknesses.

This chapter first examines some of the research on successful aging, and the elderly and education, particularly language learning. It then focuses on five organizations in different European countries that have undertaken to provide senior citizens creative, cultural, socially responsive, physically active, educational, opportunities and outlets. All of these organizations include teaching English in a meaningful and appropriate context as one of their goals.

RESEARCH ON AGING AND LEARNING

Uhlenberg (1992), a sociologist, points out that not only is the population of older people growing worldwide, many of them are well educated and have the belief that education is a lifelong process. Traditionally education has been seen as the province of young people in order to prepare them for work, because old age is a time of leisure with no expectation of social responsibility. Uhlenberg (1992) says that "since those reaching old age are increasingly well-educated, healthy, and economically secure, one might expect that they would increasingly make productive contributions to the society. But this does not appear to be happening" (p. 463). He suggests that one reason for this, besides the attitude about retirement as leisure, is that we tend to divide the life roles of education, work, and leisure by age. He suggests that the roles should be spread out throughout the lifecourse.

The social view of the one's role in different phases of life has some connection to the physical and psychological changes that occur as a person ages. Studies on cognition and memory (Backman, Small, & Wahlin, 2001; Park, 2000; Salthouse, 1996) have shown that while aging adversely affects some areas such as working memory, associative memory, incremental learning, processing speed, and the ability to focus on relevant material, "tasks involving priming, recent memory, procedural memory, and semantic memory" (Birdsong, 2006, p. 28) are less affected. "Each of these abilities is involved in some stages of L2 acquisition and routinely in language use (L1 and L2)" (p. 29). Birdsong (2006) asserts that age affects L1 (first langauge) and L2 (second language) in these areas with L2 showing effects first. Some effects are biological; others are related to "developmental aspects of cognition, L1 influence, use of the L1 and l2, and psychosocial/affective dimensions of individual's personalities, including a person's motivation to learn, appear nativelike, or integrate into L2 culture" (Birdsong , 2006, p. 36).

Other linguistic research, which is supported by neurobiological research (Knudsen, 2004), examines not just the affects of aging, but questions the critical period hypothesis. Some research shows that the critical period may be variable, that there may be "multiple critical period[s]" (Birdsong, 2006, p. 18). Research by Singleton (2005), Long (1990) and Seliger (1978) seems to support that phonological attainment may occur at a different rate and different time than "other areas of linguistic knowledge and performance" (cited in Birdsong, 2006, p. 18).

Hakuta, Bialystok, and Wiley (2003) suggested that rather than language learning being constrained at a certain age, perhaps language learning is compromised, a distinction in degree, but an important one nonetheless. They pointed out the importance of two variables on language learning: the amount of education one has, and "changes in cognition that occur with aging" (p. 32). In order to test their ideas, they analyzed data from the 1990 U.S. census on 2,016,317 Spanish-speakers and 324,444 Chinese speakers who had lived in the United States for a minimum of 10 years. They "used both 15 years and 20 years as hypothesized cutoff points for the end of the critical period" (p. 37) and performed regression analysis which tested education and age of immigration, and education, age of immigration and critical period variables. Their findings determined that there does not appear to be a specific cut-off point where second language acquisition decreases, but that it tends to steadily decline throughout the life span which they suggest is related to normal changes in cognition that occur with aging.

Rodriguez-Aranda and Martinussen (2006) in their study of L1 found that as people age, their verbal phonemic fluency decreases. It begins around 40, and increases around 60 and gains rapidly at 80. Semantic fluency also declines and there is related cognitive and working memory declines. Bellingham (2004) concluded that language learning can and does occur after 40 and that "with some careful attention to both research and informed support, the total learning experience and, as a result, the outcomes could be significantly improved for the over-40s language learner" (p. 68).

These studies recognize that while there are affects on language skills and language learning as people age, that other factors can support one's ability to learn another language at any age. Fore example, a question that this research raises is "what is successful language learning"? Traditionally second language acquisition (SLA) research has looked at adult acquisition as a failure to attain nativelike proficiency. More recent research, however, has looked at this matter from a different perspective and have used different variables, such as L1-L2 pairings (Cranshaw,

1997), increased use of L2 (Flege, Yeni-Komishian, & Liu, 1999) and motivation to sound like a native speaker (Bongaerts, 1999) and have found that "nativelikeness in late L2A [second language acquisition] is not typical, but neither is it exceedingly rare" (Dewaele, 2007, p. 20). Traditionally there has been the belief that a late learner may acquire nativelike proficiency in one or two skills but not in all (Hyltenstam & Abrahamsson, 2003; Long, 1990; Scovel, 1988). More recent research (Marinova-Todd, 2003) has shown that to the contrary some late learners can attain nativelike proficiency in a wide range of linguistic performances. Dewaele (2007) also suggests that younger learners are not as worried about making errors as older learners because they are more accustomed to the communicative approach which emphasizes "communicative competence more than ... grammatical accuracy (Stern, 1992)" (p. 405).

Physical challenges, such as hearing loss and impaired eye sight, also have an effect on an older person's ability to learn. A study by Vongpaisal and Pichora-Fuller (2007) compared hearing and vowel discrimination in younger and older adults. They found that older adults who have developed some hearing impairment do have more trouble than younger adults distinguishing between vowel sounds due to their inability to clearly hear the sounds. These findings of physical effects of aging suggest that physical aspects of aging present some of challenges that senior citizens face when learning a foreign language, in particular.

Another body of research related to learning in this age group focuses on the psychosocial perspective of successful aging. Crosnoe and Elder (2002) examined aging from the social psychological perspective and the factors that contribute to "successful aging [which] is viewed as a multifaceted phenomenon that encompasses not only health but also psychological well-being, role integration, and social engagement (Baltes & Baltes 1990; Neugarten 1969)" (p. 309). In their research, focusing on men and aging, they found that experiences throughout life influence one's "transition into the later stages of the life course" (p. 311). They make no specific connection to education, but their findings are supported by Duay and Bryan's (2006) research which did look at learning as part of the "successful aging" process.

Duay and Bryan (2006) identified a number of interrelated characteristics which contribute to successful aging, such as keeping physically and mentally active, being involved in social activities and interacting with others, maintaining independence, being open to change, "and having fun whenever possible" (p. 424). These characteristics have relevance for learning.

Participants in Duay and Bryan's (2006) study make a connection between successful aging and education in several ways. Participants reported that learning helps maintain mental alertness. One participant in Duay and Bryan's study supported the importance of activity and inter-action by commenting, "I think it is a matter of structuring your intellec-tual stimulation. It doesn't just happen watching TV or reading a book. You have to learn. You have to do things" (Duay & Bryan, 2006, p. 435). Another participant told the researchers:

> I would say keep learning things ... I find that a lot of my contemporaries who have not used or even looked into a computer or any other new devel-opments in technology—they start to become passive and want to be cared for ... I think the longer we can remain active and take initiative and try to learn, whether it's a new language or whatever it might be, that helps to stay young. (p. 435)

Duay and Bryan (2006) concluded that "interacting with others is an important aspect of what it means to be successfully aged" (p. 430). This conclusion is supported by many of the participants in their study who said that learning is "a shared experience in which the contributions of multiple parties create a more meaningful outcome for everyone involved" (p. 430). Learning is seen by many older students as mutual sharing in which everyone participates. "They want to share their ideas with others, and they want to find out what others think" (p. 437).

This type of research partially answers questions about older adult's motivations for learning a foreign language. In their research on motiva-tion for English learning among learners of different ages, Kormos and Csizér (2008) found that "older students have clear goals with language learning" (p. 347) which they say is partly attributable to older people's self-image based on their life experiences, which supports some of the general research on aging and education. Kormos and Csizér (2008) also comment that little research has been done on the motivation of adult language learners.

Older adults have a variety of motivations for learning English as a for-eign language. Some see it as good intellectual stimulation. Some learned some English earlier in life and want to continue their learning. Others go to classes because a friend is going. Some older adults may have friends and family, especially grandchildren, who live in an English-speaking country. Their motivation is to be better able to communicate with them.

In a study conducted in the United States with older adults who were learning English as a Second Language (ESL), the participants identified three motivations for learning English: integration into American society; engagement in meaningful communication; and being autonomous (Hubenthal, 2004). These learners were university educated Russian-speaking immigrants from the former Soviet Union and the 10 partici-pants were in their late 60s and early 70s. The subcategories they identified as barriers to their successful acquisition of English skills despite systematic study were memory, aging, shame, health problems, lack of accessible ESL courses, and the Russian social context in which they grew up.

Even though these learners had the added motivation of wanting to integrate into the society in which they were living, many of their issues were similar to those of other older people in an EFL language learning situation. No matter their motivation and desire to learn, the social issue that is similar in many countries and societies: the elderly are marginalized and are not offered opportunities outside of traditional roles.

THE OPEN-GATE PROJECT

However, due to the factors enumerated by Uhlenberg (1992), some older citizens in countries around the world have taken on the task of creating their own opportunities. They have joined and founded organizations whose goals are to provide senior citizens with more opportunities for meaningful educational experiences and for greater involvement in society. Five of these organizations have reached beyond the borders of their country and are part of a group called The Open-Gate. The two goals of the Open-Gate are to help older adults enhance their computer skills and to improve their English language skills. The five organizations are: The Adult Education Center in Finland, UNIEDA (the Italian Adult Education Union), the UTA in the Czech Republic, Las Rosas School in Spain, and Akademia Pełni Życia in Poland.

The mission of the Open Gate is to establish mutual cooperation and understanding between European Union (EU) countries. They acknowledge that citizens of the EU must be citizens of their nation as well as the larger community that forms the EU. Regular electronic communication and yearly seminars, all conducted in English, are intended to provide space for mutual sharing. The five groups that make up Open-Gate each have English courses as one of their offerings to their members.

The Adult Education Center, Vaasa, Finland

The Adult Education Center in Vaasa, Finland was established in response to the growing numbers of seniors in Finland. The group states that at the same time, there is a decrease in the feeling of community in many areas and that the "generations are growing apart from each other" (Open Gate-Finland, n.d., para. 1). The center aims to help seniors develop a stronger sense of community and connectedness, while empowering them to participate more fully in society. The center helps them learn new techniques of self-expression and give them opportunities for connecting with people locally and abroad. Membership in the Open-Gate project is one of these opportunities. The center offers a beginning level and intermediate level English course to its members so they can more fully participate in this project. You can find information about The Adult Education Center at these two websites:

- http://opengate.felk.cvut.cz/partners/finland_cz.html and
- http://vaasagate.blogspot.com/2009/04/aims-of-open-gate-project-enhancing.html

UNIEDA (the Italian Adult Education Union), Rome, Italy

The UNIEDA is "an umbrella organisation, whose members (currently 60) are Popular Universities, Third Age Universities and Italian cultural associations" (Open Gate-Italy, n.d., para. 1). Therefore UNIEDA does not focus only on the needs of senior citizens, but citizens of all ages who are considered in disadvantaged in some way, such as learners with special needs, and migrants. The group in Rome offers an upper intermediate level English course for its members. Their link in Open-Gate is:

- http://opengate.felk.cvut.cz/partners/italy_cz.html

UTA, Czech Republic

The UTA is designed for citizens "who belong to disadvantaged and vulnerable groups in the present- day modern society" (Open Gate-Czech, n.d., para. 1) such as senior citizens. Its approach to teaching is designed with these learners in mind, so they can enhance their knowledge. Their English course is geared for all levels, and has a special focus on English for use in talking about and using information technology, science and culture. Learn more about them at:

- http://opengate.felk.cvut.cz/partners/czech_cz.html

Las Rosas School, Madrid, Spain

The Las Rosas School in Spain is also a member of the Open-Gate project. They offer basic education services to a variety of groups of people including migrants, school drop-outs, learners who have special needs, and people who for some reason had little or no access to educational opportunities, as well as senior citizens. They focus on developing basic computer skills for seniors so that they can better function in today's society. The aims of their English courses are for their students to be able to communicate with those in other countries to learn about them and to teach others about Spain. Their website is:

- http://www.educa.madrid.org/web/cepa.lasrosas.madrid/ open%20gate/index.html

Akademia Pełni Życia, Krakow, Poland

The final group is one that I am personally familiar with. The Akademia Pełni Życia (APZ), the Fullness-of-Life Academy, is a nonprofit organization run by and for senior citizens.

APZ was established when the woman is now the director realized that there was a need for computer training for older adults. According to their website:

We put special emphasis on giving senior citizens, access to modern computer technology and the achievements of contemporary science and culture. We also aim at changing the negative stereotypes concerning the position and role of elderly people in society, as well as changing their own attitude towards their maturity and age. We strive to create a new image of a Pensioner, who would be up-to-date, independent, and willingly and actively participating in the modern world.

APZ offers computer classes, language courses, lectures, seminars, discussion groups, clubs, and hobby groups. The computer and English courses are taught by a small paid staff. However, many of these activities are organized and run by the members themselves. Even though members have to pay a fee, APZ's computer classes and English classes always have waiting lists. The computer classes for seniors have been so successful that the director and her staff are often asked to speak not only about how they have created such a successful grassroots organization, but how they teach computer skills to seniors effectively. You can read more about them at:

- http://opengate.felk.cvut.cz/partners/poland_cz.html   and   http://apz.org.pl/pokaz/in_english

CONCLUSION

My association with APZ is what actually got me interested in this topic. Before this I had never really thought about what people in other countries do once they get older. Many of the older people that I know in the United States lead fairly fulfilling lives. In the United States there are community colleges which offer courses for people of all ages. Religious organizations often have programs for older people with speakers and programs on topics of interest to older people. Many older people do meaningful volunteer work. However, traditionally in Poland (and other European countries) older people, especially older women, are burdened with the stereotype of the old granny wearing the babushka, sitting by the fire, and taking care of the grandchildren.

According to research, because their motivations for learning differ from those of younger people, "older adults prefer programs that stimulate curiosity and provide personally relevant content" (Duay & Bryan, 2006, p. 440). Based on research by Knowles (1980), Duay and Bryan (2006) say that "To keep older adults excited and interested in what they are learning, adult educators need to design courses that teach knowledge and skills within a meaningful and useful context" (p. 440).

Organizations such as those who are part of the Open-Gate Project offer this type of meaningful and useful context. The members are active and engaged in numerous activities at home and abroad which require their use of English, giving them an authentic motivation for language learning. The groups work on projects that have relevance for the members as active participants in the modern world.

One day when I was at APZ, a woman explained to me how incensed she was that she has been working so hard to break the stereotypes of seniors and that they are still being perpetuated. Her grandson's school had sent home a photo for Grandparent's Day which was in a frame showing a stereotypical "babcia and dziadek (granny and grandpa)." She told me quite definitely, "I am very busy and I do not have time to sit and knit!"

REFERENCES

Backman, L., Small, B., & Wahlin, A. (2001). Aging and memory: Cognitive and biological perspectives. In J. E. Birren & K. W. Schaie (Eds.), *Handbook of the psychology of aging* (5th ed., pp. 349-377). San Diego, CA: Academic Press.

Baltes, P., & Baltes, M. (Eds.). (1990). Psychological perspectives on successful aging: The model of selective optimization with compensation. In *Successful aging: Perspectives from the behavioral sciences* (pp. 1-34). New York, NY: Cambridge University Press.

Bellingham, L. (2004). Is there language acquisition after 40: Older learners speak up. In P. Benson & D. Nunan (Eds.), *Learners' stories: Difference and diversity in language learning* (pp. 56-68). Cambridge, England: Cambridge University Press.

Birdsong, D. (2006). Age and second language acquisition and processing: A selective overview. *Language Learning Supplement, 56*, 9-49.

Bongaerts, T. (1999). Ultimate attainment in L2 pronunciation: The case of very advanced late learners. In D. Birdsong (Ed.), *Second language acquisition and the critical period hypothesis* (pp. 133-159). Mahwah, NJ: Erlbaum.

Cranshaw, A. (1997). *A study of Anglophone native and near-native linguistic and meta-linguistics performance*. Unpublished doctoral dissertation, Universite de Montreal, Montreal, Canada.

Crosnoe, R., & Elder, G., Jr. (2002). Successful adaptation in the later years: A life course approach to aging. *Social Psychology Quarterly, 65*(4), 309-328.

Dewaele, J. (2007). The effect of multilingualism, sociobiographical, and situational factor on communicative anxiety and foreign language anxiety of mature language learners. *International Journal of Bilingualism, 11*(4), 391-409.

Duay, D., & Bryan, V. (2006). Senior adults' perceptions of successful aging. *Educational Gerontology, 32*(6), 423-445.

Flege, J. (2002). No perfect bilinguals. In A. James & J. Leather (Eds.), *New sounds 2000: Proceedings of the Fourth International Symposium on the Acquisition of Second-Language Speech* (pp. 132-141). Austria: University of Klagenfurt.

Flege, J. E., Yeni-Komshian, G. H., & Liu, S. (1999). Age constraints on second-language acquisition. *Journal of Memory and Language, 41*, 78-104.

Hakuta, K., Bialystok, E., & Wiley, E. (2003). Critical evidence: A test of the Critical-Period Hypothesis for second-language acquisition. *Psychological Science, 14*(1), 31-38.

Hubenthal, W. (2004). Older Russian immigrants' experiences in learning English: Motivation, methods, and barriers. *Adult Basic Education, 14*(2), 104-126.

Hyltenstam, K., & Abrahamsson, N. (2003). Maturational constraints in SLA. In C. J. Doughy & M. H. Long (Eds.), *The handbook of second language acquisition* (pp. 539-588). Malden, MA: Blackwell.

Knowles, M. (1980). *The modern practice of adult education: From pedagogy to andragogy* (2nd ed.). New York, NY: Cambridge Books.

Knudsen, E. (2004). Sensitive periods in the development of the brain and behavior. *Journal of Cognitive Neuroscience, 16*(8), 1412-1425.

Kormos, J., & Csizér, K. (2008). Age-related differences in the motivation of learning English as a foreign language: Attitudes, selves, and motivated learning behavior. *Language Learning, 58*(2), 327-55.

Long, M. (1990). Maturational constraints on language development. *Studies in Second Language Acquisition, 12*(3), 251-285.

Marinova-Todd, S. (2003). *Comprehensive analysis of ultimate attainment in adult second language acquisition*. Unpublished doctoral dissertation, Harvard University.

Neugarten, B. (1969). Continuities and discontinuities of psychological issues into adult life. *Human Development 12*, 121-130.

Open Gate-Czech Republic. (n.d.). *Finland*. Retrieved from http://opengate .felk.cvut.cz/partners/czech_cz.html

Open Gate-Finland. (n.d.). *Finland*. Retrieved from http://opengate.felk.cvut.cz/ partners/finland_cz.html

Open Gate-Italy. (n.d.). *Finland*. Retrieved from http://opengate.felk.cvut.cz /partners/italy_cz.html

Park, D. C. (2000). The basic mechanisms accounting for age-related decline in cognitive function. In D. C. Park & N. Schwartz (Eds.), *Cognitive aging: A primer* (pp. 3-21). Philadelphia, PA: Psychology Press.

Rodriguez-Aranda, C., & Martinussen, M. (2006). Age-related differences in performance of phonemic verbal fluency measured by Controlled Oral Word Association Task (COWAT): A meta-analytic study. *Developmental Neuropsychology, 30*(2), 697-717.

Salthouse, T. A. (1996). Constraints on theories of cognitive aging. *Psychonomic Bulletin & Review, 3*(3), 287-299.

Scovel, T. (1988). *A time to speak: A psycholinguistic inquiry into the critical period for human speech.* Rowley, MA: Newbury House.

Seliger, H. W. (1978). Implications of a multiple critical periods hypothesis for second language learning. In W. Ritchie (Ed.), *Second language acquisition research: Issues and implications* (pp. 11-19). New York, NY: Academic Press.

Singleton, D. (2005). The critical period hypothesis: A coat of many colours. *International review of Applied Linguistics, 43*(4), 269-286.

Stern, H. (1992). *Issues and options in language teaching.* Oxford, England: Oxford University Press.

Uhlenberg, P. (1992). Population aging and social policy. *Annual Review of Sociology, 1992, 18*, 449-474.

Vongpaisal, T., & Pichora-Fuller, K. (2007). Effect of age on F_0 difference limen and concurrent vowel identification. *Journal of Speech, Hearing, and Language Research, 50*, 1139-1156.

REFLECTION QUESTIONS

1. How can knowledge about the effects of aging help a teacher better plan for teaching English to this age group?

2. What are other issues that might be of importance to be aware of when working with this age group?

3. How are issues different in the ESL and EFL contexts?

FOLLOW-UP ACTIVITIES

1. Interview a teacher who works with older adults.

2. Investigate what types of foreign language and ESL programs there are in your community for senior citizens.

FURTHER READING

- Muñoz, C. (Ed.). (2006). *Age and the rate of foreign language learning.* Clevedon, United Kingdom: Multilingual Matters.
- Perry, F. L., Jr. (2005). *Research in applied linguistics: Becoming a discerning consumer.* Mahwah, NJ: Erlbaum.

PART III

Educational Reform
and English Language Teaching

OVERVIEW

Educational reform in the United States in recent years has taken several forms, some intended for implementation at the school or district level, while some have aimed at students themselves. For example, the U.S. Department of Education has put federal programs, such as Title I, in place to provide aid to poor and low-performing students. School choice in the form of vouchers and charter schools were designed to give parents choices where to send their children, to allow parents to remove their students from poorly performing schools. The increase of affordable and accessible technology has also brought about changes in the way schools approach teaching and learning. However, the most visible and probably the most controversial reform in the late twentieth century in American schools years is the increase in standardized testing.

In 1983 the National Commission for Excellence in Education in its report *A Nation at Risk: The Imperative for Educational Reform,* declared that American schools were failing. They reported on everything from low literacy rates to an inability to compute simple math problems. Improving

ESL, EFL, and Bilingual Education: Exploring Historical, Sociocultural, Linguistic, and Instructional Foundations, pp. 105–107
Copyright © 2010 by Information Age Publishing

education quickly became a political issue that spawned a variety of reforms. In the wave of educational reform that took hold in the 1990s, standardized testing became high-stakes testing, used as the measure of not only how well students were performing but how well schools were performing. In an effort to hold schools and teachers accountable for the failure of students, students' score on a battery of standardized tests have become the focal point. One of the effects of this emphasis on testing is that schools and teachers began reshaping their curriculum to match what is on the test, so that the curriculum has narrowed so that they are teaching to the test. Another effect is that these multiple choice tests tend to be aimed at superficial reasoning rather than critical thinking skills. Therefore, critics say that not only are students being taught less, they are also not being taught problem-solving and critical thinking skills that are necessary for their intellectual development.

Peterson and Neill (1999) suggested that assessment should more complex than relying on one test score.

> The challenge is to match assessment that is integrated into classroom instruction, and is focused primarily on helping individual children, with assessment that provides school- and district-wide information being demanded by local and state officials or various community forces. (para. 4)

Rather than being punitive and focusing on what students do not know, testing which is used for school assessment should focus on what the students do know and how to help them learn better. Alternative assessments should be developed which serve a specific purpose, not the one-size fits all model of standardized testing. Besides assessments which measure what students are learning, there should be assessments which serve other purposes, such as how well the schools are "providing equal opportunity to all students ... the effectiveness of various programs ... how well they are spending taxpayers' money ... to report to parents, or summarize and certify a student's achievement ... to help transform the curriculum. (Peterson & Neill, 1999, para. 7)

Educational reform should be focused on improving education for the students in any country. However, oftentimes what is considered improvement is driven by political, economic, and social agendas that may or may not be in the best interests of all students.

- Chapter 9: "No Child Left Behind and English Language Learners: Issues in Assessment" focuses on standardized testing as a form of assessment and its impact on bilingual/ESL education.
- Chapter 10: "Educational and Curricular Reforms in Latvia and Poland: Perspectives of Pre-Service English Teachers" compares data from research on educational reforms in Poland and Latvia

and how they affect the perspectives of pre-service teachers of English. (Originally published: Zimmerman, L. (2008). Educational and curricular reforms in Latvia and Poland: Perspectives of pre-service English teachers. *World Studies in Education, 9*(2): 83-101.)

- Chapter 11: "Teaching Bilingual Students with Special Needs: A Teacher Training Issue" compares data in the research literature of effectively educating bilingual/ESL students with special needs. (Originally published: Zimmerman, L. (2008). Teaching bilingual students with special needs: A teacher training issue. *i-manager's Journal on Educational Psychology, 2*(2), 21-25. Reprinted with permission of the publisher.)

REFERENCES

Peterson, B., & Neill, M. (1999). Alternative to standardized tests. *Rethinking Schools 13*(3). Retrieved from http://www.rethinkingschools.org/archive/13_03/assess.shtml

CHAPTER 9

NO CHILD LEFT BEHIND AND ENGLISH LANGUAGE LEARNERS

Issues in Assessment

Educational reform as mandated by the No Child Left Behind Act (NCLB) has the potential to improve the education of all children in the United States. However, because the legislation does not make a clear distinction between school assessment and individual student assessment, the educational issues that English Language Learners (ELLs) face are not being addressed adequately. Standardized testing, in particular, is problematic. A study of the literature about standardized assessment and ELLs reveals that although NCLB's goal is to ensure quality and equitable education for all students in American schools, it falls short, and in some instances actually creates an inequitable learning environment for some students. Despite the pressure of high-stakes testing, the teacher's role when working with ELLs must go beyond preparing them to take tests to meet NCLB standards, to preparing them to be successful in all aspects of life in the United States. As standardized tests become more widespread internationally, the issues faced in the United States can be seen as a indicator of what is becoming a global issue.

ESL, EFL, and Bilingual Education: Exploring Historical, Sociocultural, Linguistic, and Instructional Foundations, pp. 109–119
Copyright © 2010 by Information Age Publishing

This chapter first examines assessment focusing on standardized testing as a form of assessment. Then it summarizes NCLB legislation, examining the implications of federal education standards and standardized testing for students who are ELL. Finally, it offers some suggestions how teachers can use assessment strategies to support these students while preparing them for success in American schools.

ASSESSMENT BASICS

Assessment serves several functions in the educational setting to determine what students know and what they can do. Standardized tests are generally summative assessments which are norm-referenced, comparing each test-taker's score to that of all other test-takers. According to Brown (2003), a standardized test "presupposes standard objectives or criteria [and] standard procedures for administration and scoring" (p. 67). Standardized tests are usually multiple choice tests that can be scored easily using automated scoring systems, and can be administered efficiently to large numbers of students. Although supporters of standardized tests argue that they are both valid and reliable, one of the strongest arguments for using them is this practicality.

ELLs are confronted with having to take standardized tests designed to assess their language ability, as well as the high-stakes NCLB mandated tests. Despite being considered reliable and practical, standardized tests present ELLs with several challenges, including cultural bias, decontextualization, and inadequate feedback (Ariza, Morales-Jones, Yahya, & Zainuddin, 2002).

Cultural bias within testing instruments can wrongly evaluate a student's knowledge. Although standardized tests are norm-referenced, they can behave like criterion-based tests if background knowledge comes into play in the test items, as when items are based in a particular cultural perspective, or when the test delivery strategy is unfamiliar (Ariza et al., 2002). For example, a multiple choice test question asks about the number of candles on a birthday cake. If the student is unfamiliar with this cultural icon, they can misinterpret the question, and the multiple choice type of question is biased toward students for whom this is a familiar testing strategy. Rather than being a test of student knowledge of content, the test becomes a test of the student's cultural knowledge, and/or test-taking ability.

Related to the issue of cultural bias is the notion that all ELLs are treated as though they have similar backgrounds and are linguistically homogeneous (Solano-Flores, 2008). ELLs, even within one classroom, may come from a variety of linguistic backgrounds, have "different migration histories, different kinds of exposure to formal instruction both in L1 [first language] and L2 [second language]" (Solano-Flores 2008, p. 189). These and other social, linguistic, and cultural factors are often ignored when making decisions about their education, including assessment. In Solano-Flores' (2008) review of research surrounding ELLs and assessment, the author contends that standardized language assessments of ELLs are rarely "comprehensive enough to provide an accurate picture of proficiency in both L1 and L2 and in the four language modes ... [providing] fragmented and inconsistent information about the linguistic proficiency of ELLs" (p. 190).

Standardized tests tend to fragment knowledge, and to present decontextualized test items. A teacher-designed assessment, whether a multiple choice test, an essay, or oral, can be tailored to content and language that the teacher knows that students have been exposed to. Since there is no nationally standardized curriculum in the United States, the content of a standardized test may or may not be relevant to what the students have been learning. However, with the consequences of high-stakes standardized testing looming over them, many educators worry that if they do not "teach to the test," they and their students will fail (Richard-Amato, 2003). Many standardized tests assess content knowledge, with little or no context, and ask questions which involve little or no critical thinking (Ariza et al., 2002), with right and wrong answers which may depend on knowledge that the ELL does not have. For example, a question may use a grammatical construction that the learners have not learned yet, resulting in a wrong answer. The test then becomes a grammar test for the students, rather than testing knowledge of content, making it neither a valid test of their knowledge nor useful for their learning.

Assessment must be carefully designed so that it measures what it is designed to measure. When planning assessment for students who are ELL content and language must be considered (Ariza et al., 2002; Richard-Amato, 2003). Determining what content to assess is usually straightforward. What did the student learn about the presented material or from the assignment? However, with language, what is being measured becomes more complex. Research has shown that ELLs "may show improvement in content knowledge (such as math) only when their level of academic English proficiency increases"(Abedi, 2004, p. 7) which raises the question of the validity of standardized assessments for ELLs. In a classroom setting, where the teacher has control over assessment, the teacher can be careful to use constructions and vocabulary on the test with which the student is familiar and not make assumptions about their language skills. For example, in the lesson, the students learned: The influence of the government's policy is important. If the test question says: What weight does the government's policy carry? a student not familiar with this construction will not realize that "carry weight" is synonymous with "influence." A university student who immigrated to the United States from Serbia said that when she was in high school, she would become paralyzed when she read a test question that included a name that she did not recognize, such as: If Tracy has three apples and gives John one, how many apples are left? She would get hung up on not knowing whether Tracy was a boy or a girl, and would not be able to solve the problem (personal communication, February 22, 2006). Her inability to solve the problem was directly related to language issues not her math-solving ability.

Washback is another issue that has positive and negative implications for assessment and for the language learner (Brown, 2003). The negative factors include teaching factors, such as the teacher narrowing the curriculum to teach only what will be tested, or spending more time teaching test-taking strategies than teaching content. However, washback can have positive effects when used as feedback by helping students and teachers pinpoint areas of difficulty. With teacher-designed tests, and other tests administered within the classroom, the teacher and students have opportunities for isolating student strengths and weaknesses. However, standardized tests administered on a large scale offer little or no feedback (Ariza et al., 2002), so that the students and the teacher never know if the student missed the questions due to lack of content knowledge or lack of appropriate linguistic abilities.

Even standardized language tests which are designed specifically for ELLs can pose challenges. A kindergarten teacher said that she was curious about the difficulty of the standardized test she was required to administer to the ELLs in her kindergarten class (personal communication, November 19, 2006). She asked one of her "brighter" native-English speaking students to take the test, and after completing it, he told her it was hard. She realized that even though the test was designed for ELLs, it probably was not an appropriate measure of their language abilities. Her conclusion is not surprising when one considers that standardized tests are usually field tested with native English speakers who can understand more complex linguistic structures than ELLs (TESOL, 2005).

STANDARDS AND NO CHILD LEFT BEHIND (NCLB)

Standards of learning are important in order to ensure that children receive an equitable education and that they learn what they need to in order to be productive and successful members of society. "Standards specify what students should know and what they should be able to do" (Richard-Amato, 2003, p. 146), providing a framework for curriculum development, and for assessment of students and programs. Although

NCLB's aim is to use standards-based learning and assessment to ensure teacher and school accountability so that all children receive an equitable education, its ultimate result has been to redefine the focus of schooling in the United States.

NCLB is one in a series of federal mandates to provide equitable education for all students in American schools by requiring states to provide high standards for academic content and to develop valid and reliable assessments aligned with these standards (Abedi et al., 2004). Title III of the NCLB Act specifically addresses the education of ELLs.

> "The major goals of Title III are to help ensure that limited English proficient children attain English proficiency, develop high levels of academic competence in English, and meet the same challenging state academic content and students achievement standards" as all other students. States are required to develop English language proficiency standards and implement English proficiency tests. They must also develop annual achievement objectives for increasing the English language proficiency of ELLs and assessing their progress in speaking, reading, writing, listening, and comprehension. State language proficiency assessments must be linked to state academic standards. (Miller, 2003, p. 1)

NCLB originally specified that students who have been in the United States for 3 or more years must be tested in English and language arts (Miller-Whitehead, 2005). That timeframe has been reduced to 1 year. The Center for Public Education (2007) reports that "ELLs are tested in math starting with the first round of state exams after the student enters school [and] are tested in reading that year or the following year" (para. 4).

Therefore, in addition to any English language proficiency standardized test that ELLs may have to take, they and their teachers in American schools are also responsible for their taking standardized achievement tests mandated by NCLB. Any social, cultural, linguistic, or other factors that are evidenced in English proficiency standardized tests are amplified. The students must know the content as well as be able to read and answer questions about the content in a language in which they may be more or less proficient.

Despite research showing that using multiple types of assessments are more reliable and more valid measures of student achievement than using a single type (Loadman & Thomas, n.d.), NCLB has mandated a narrow form of assessment, a rigid system of high-stakes standardized testing. Not only is just one type of assessment used, but the results of these assessments carry heavy penalties for schools whose students do not perform well on these tests.

Relying solely on one type of assessment is inherently discriminatory. In this climate, the student who is an English-learner becomes a liability to the school. When ELLs walk into an American classroom, they bring a language, a culture, and a set of beliefs, values, and expectations that make up their identities. In an ideal situation, the classroom is a place where the whole person is respected and nurtured. However, in reality, the child's identity is often fragmented and compartmentalized. They are seen as a student who does not speak English, as a person from another country or culture, as someone different from the "norm." If their culture and values are considered at all, they are seen in light of difference from everyone else, not as what makes them who they are. They are identified as: ESL student; LEP student; immigrant student. Rather than focusing on what they can do, the student who speaks Spanish and is learning English, school classifications focus on "deficiencies." This fragmentation and focus on deficiencies is important to consider when looking at standardized testing mandated by NCLB, and its expectations of and effects on these students.

In the present climate of standards-driven education, the standards have taken on more importance than the learning itself and the students who are being educated. To be effective standards should be based on students' needs rather than students' needs being shaped by the standards. Rather than seeing students as individuals with diverse needs and abilities, standards-driven education assumes that all students learn the same content at the same rate in the same way (Amorosino, 2006; Valinski, 2006), measuring all students regardless of needs by the same yardstick.

Standards are also being used to measure school and teacher performance. Educators' jobs and schools are at risk if students perform poorly on these standardized tests, so that standards have become tools of punishment for low-performing schools, the schools and students who need the most help, rather than serving as guidelines to improve education. Schools with large populations of non-English speaking students, are at a disadvantage with standards that do not take language differences into account, are often located in urban areas without the resources to adequately meet their students' needs.

These stringent requirements have been contested by a number of people as being unreasonable and unattainable for many ELLs, and for their schools (Abedi, 2004; Loadman & Thomas, n.d.; Valinski, 2006). Consequently, a few concessions have been made regarding alternative assessments, and other accommodations, but overall the standardized tests stand as the only means of assessment. Accommodations for ELLs are "changes in the test process, in the test itself, or in the test response format" (Abedi, Hofstetter, & Lord, 2004, p. 2). However, they must be carefully designed to ensure that they do not give ELLs "an advantage over students who do not receive the accommodation" (Abedi et al., 2004, p. 2). NCLB also has the caveat that if "only one half of 1% of students in any subgroup can be tested using alternative assessment, unless the group is too small to obtain statistically reliable results" (Miller-Whitehead, 2005, p. 3).

SUPPORTING ELLS USING ASSESSMENT STRATEGIES

There is an upside, however, to this concern with standards and standardization. Being explicit about what children need to learn in order to do well on the tests supports Delpit's (1993) contention that the rules should be taught to and made explicit to students who do not grow up as part of the dominant society.

> The children who are part of that [dominant] culture have an immediate advantage in the educational arena, because they have the "cultural capital" needed for success. They understand the stated and unstated rules of being in this group or society" (Zimmerman, 2007, p. 22)

Bohn and Sleeter (2000) contend that "standards make visible the expectations for learning that otherwise were implicit" (p. 60).

Valinski (2006) points out that, despite the problems with NCLB, it has brought about some improvements for ELLs. NCLB ensures that ELLs are no longer ignored in the classroom; their academic needs must be recognized and met. The curriculum for ELLs is being better defined, so that students are learning English in an academic, content-based context. The focus on testing and the high-stakes related to test results have encouraged teachers to use assessment results to try help students perform better, which has impacted ELLs' learning of English as well as content. Farhady (1982) suggests that positive feedback could be enhanced by providing detailed score reporting giving teachers more open access to their students' test results.

Student success is dependent on a number of variables. The teacher and school can provide the conditions that students need for success, such as a comfortable learning environment, adequate supplies and resources, appropriate equipment, expectations for success and culturally responsive teaching and assessment strategies (Altschuler & Schmautz, 2006; Ariza et al., 2002; Richard-Amato, 2003). However, by focusing on standardized tests as the only way of measuring student growth, educators are being forced to ignore a body of research which has demonstrated that different assessments measure various skills and knowledge (Ariza et al., 2002; Richard-Amato, 2003). A variety of authentic assessments which represent realistic situations and conditions, such as self-assessment, peer feedback, and teacher evaluation, can demonstrate that students are meeting educational standards (Ariza et al., 2002). Designed by teachers who know the students' needs, they are valid reflections of students' learning, and are linguistically appropriate for the learners. Authentic assessments are not always practical, as they can be time-intensive, but their usefulness as learning tools is supported by research data (Ariza et al., 2002; Richard-Amato, 2003).

However, since high-stakes standardized tests are the reality, educators must look at what can be done to help ELLs be successful. Use of accommodations as allowed by the legislation is one effective strategy. To ensure validity, accommodations must be individualized for each student, since each English learner's ability to use language differs. For a student with fairly high English skills, extended time might be a sufficient accommodation, whereas for one with lower skills, extra time would serve no purpose; however, a special glossary might be a useful tool for this student. Research has shown that "modifying the language but not the content of the test item" (Abedi et al., 2004, p. 17) is a very effective accommodation and one which is rarely used. Although Solano-Flores (2008) questions how effective such accommodations are if not implemented equitably, modifications to the language of the test can "reduce the level of unnecessary linguistic complexity and cultural bias" (Abedi & Dietel, 2004, p. 785), thereby improving the performance of ELLs by as much as 10-20%.

However, Kieffer, Lesaux, Rivera, and Francis (2009) state that "accommodations are largely ineffective in improving the performance of the majority of ELLs on large-scale assessments" (p. 1190), even accommodations such as using an English dictionary or glossary which are somewhat effective. They suggest that rather than focusing on accommodations, educators should focus on ensuring that students receive direct instruction of relevant academic English as well as appropriate content instruction in their native language.

NCLB has provided professional development funding (Valinski, 2006), so teachers and schools should take advantage of opportunities to learn how to work more effectively with ELLs. Strategies such as differentiated instruction and differentiated assessment can positively impact students' learning and proficiency. These and other integrated instructional strategies can allow for assessment which is embedded in instruction (Brown, 2003; Gibbons, 2002). Rather than taking away time from classroom instruction, assessment embedded in coursework will provide opportunities for assessment which are valid, reliable, and useful, while preparing the students for success on high-stakes tests as well as in the classroom.

Farhady (2008 lecture notes) suggests that changes on the macrolevel, changes to the standardized testing paradigm itself, could enhance student success. Changes in test design so that samples of students' linguistic performance vary widely and so that what samples will be gathered are unpredictable, as well as using more open-ended test items will provide more validity to standardized tests. As Farhady suggests, more research must be conducted on the "predictive validity studies of public exams [and] insure that each exam board has a research capacity" (p. 3) in order to provide ELLS with equitable standardized testing, and an equitable learning environment.

CONCLUSION

Standardized testing is used in a number of ways to assess ELLs, from placement in English classes to the high-stakes testing mandated by NCLB. Because of the weight that it carries, this high-stakes standardized assessment has serious ramifications for ELLs. According to Altschuler and Schmautz (2006), academic performance is directly related to academic self-concept and self-efficacy. Students who perform poorly on standardized tests tend "to judge themselves as having less ability than students with higher scores" (Altschuler & Schmautz, 2006, p. 9). A student's performing poorly on a standardized test can result in underachievement, decreased self-esteem, and resistance, which can be manifested in various kinds of acting out (Altshuler & Schmautz, 2006). The long-term results may be that these students lose interest in education, ultimately resulting in lack of success in school, even lack of completion, thereby negatively impacting their chances for success later in life. However, well-designed and academically appropriate assessments, which adequately measure student achievement, can provide support and encouragement for the student's academic growth and success.

Research and anecdotal evidence by educators in the field have demonstrated that a variety of assessment strategies allow for comprehensive evaluation of "student knowledge, skills, and abilities" (Loadman & Thomas, n.d., p. 1), giving the clearest picture of student learning. Despite the pressure of high-stakes testing, the teacher's role when working with ELLs must go beyond preparing them to take tests so that they can meet NCLB standards. They must also be prepared to be successful in all aspects of life.

REFERENCES

Abedi, J. (2004). The No Child Left Behind Act and English language learners: Assessment and accountability issues. *Educational Researcher, 33*(1), 4-14.

Abedi, J., & Dietl, R. (2004). Challenges in the No Child Left Behind Act for English-language learners. *Phi Delta Kappan, 85*(10), 782-785.

Abedi, J., Hofstetter, C. H., & Lord, C. (2004). Assessment accommodations for English language learners: Implications for policy-based empirical research. *Review of Educational Research, 74*(1), 1-28.

Altschuler, S. J., & Schmautz, T. (2006). No Hispanic student left behind: The consequences of "high stakes" testing. *Children & Schools, 28*(1), 5-14.

Amorosino, C. (2006). *No Child Left Behind: Ensuring high academic achievement for Limited English Proficient students and students with disabilities.* Testimony to the House Committee on Education and the Workforce. Retrieved from www.tesol.org

Ariza, E., Morales-Jones, C., Yahya, N., & Zainuddin, H. (2002). *Why TESOL? Theories and issues in Teaching English as a second language with a K-12 focus* (2nd ed.). Dubuque, IA: Kendall/Hunt.

Bohn, A., & Sleeter, C. (2001). Will multicultural education survive the standards movement? [Electronic version]. *Education Digest, 66*(5), 17-24. Retrieved from Academic Search Premier.

Brown, H. D. (2003). *Language assessment: Principles and classroom practices.* White Plains, NY: Longman.

Center for Public Education. (2007). *What NCLB says about ELL students.* Retrieved from http://www.centerforpubliceducation.org/site/c.kjJXJ5MPIwE/b .3532065/k.51B7/What_NCLB_says_about_ELL_students.htm

Delpit, L. (1993). *Other people's children: Cultural conflict in the classroom.* New York, NY: The New Press.

Farhady, H. (1982). Measures of language proficiency from the learners' perspective. *TESOL Quarterly, 16*(1), 43-59.

Gibbons, P. (2002). *Scaffolding language, scaffolding learning: Teaching second language learners in the mainstream classroom.* Portsmouth, NH: Heinemann.

Kieffer, M., Lesaux, N., Rivera, M., & Francis, D. (2009). Accommodations for English language learners taking large-scale assessments: A meta-analysis on effectiveness and validity. *Review of Educational Research, 79*(3), 1168-1201.

Loadman, W. E., & Thomas, A. M. (n.d.). *Standardized test scores and alternative assessment: Different pieces of the same puzzle.* Retrieved from www.enc.org/topics/ assessment/testing/document.shtm

Miller, K. (2003, Fall). English language learners and the No Child Left Behind Act. *Changing Schools.* Aurora CO: MCREL. (ERIC Document Reproduction Service No. ED 482 752).

Miller-Whitehead, M. (2005, January). *Why measuring growth is especially important in evaluation of English Language Learners.* Paper presented at the annual meeting of AMTESOL. (ERIC Document Reproduction Service No. ED 490 539).

Richard-Amato, P. (2003). *Making it happen: From interactive to participatory language teaching* (3rd ed.). White Plains, NY: Longman.

Solano-Flores, G. (2008). Who is given tests in what language by whom, when, and where? The need for probabilistic views of language in the testing of English language learners. *Educational Researcher, 37*(4), 189-199.

TESOL. (2005). Position paper on assessment and accountability of English Language Learners under the No Child Left Behind Act of 2001 (Public Law 107-110). Retrieved from www.tesol.org

Valinski, S. (2006). *The impact of NCLB on English language learners. TESOL Testifies Before NCLB Commission*. Retrieved November 13, 2007 from www.tesol.org

Zimmerman, L. W. (2007). Culture of silence: The complicity of American education. *Journal of Contemporary Educational Issues, 3*(1), 22-26.

REFLECTION QUESTIONS

1. What kind of learning are standardized tests useful for measuring?
2. What is the rationale of measuring a school's success based on the standardized test scores of its students? How is this a valid measure? Or not?
3. How can authentic assessment be used to accomplish the same goals as standardized testing? Or can it?

FOLLOW-UP ACTIVITIES

1. Look up the test scores and AYP (Annual Yearly Progress) reports of schools in your area. What factors in the community contribute to the scores?
2. Interview an administrator of a "failing" school about the issues he or she sees as influencing the school's and students' performance.

FURTHER READING

Brown, H. D. (2003). *Language assessment: Principles and classroom practices*. White Plains, NY: Longman.

Menendez, R. (Director). (1988). *Stand and deliver* [Motion picture]. United States: Warner Brothers.

CHAPTER 10

EDUCATIONAL AND CURRICULAR REFORMS IN LATVIA AND POLAND

Perspectives of Preservice English Teachers

INTRODUCTION

The recent transitions in the political and economic structures in Poland and Latvia have affected the society in both countries. Changes in a society generally result in educational reform, which can be a complex undertaking. Reform may involve curriculum changes at the local and national level; transformations in the structure of schools; differences in the ways that assessment and evaluation are carried out; changes in administration; and modifications in the education of teachers, and those who are studying to be teachers (preservice teachers) and those who are already teaching (in-service teachers). This qualitative research project focuses on how preservice English teachers in Latvia and Poland perceive their roles as future teachers in the particular context of their societies, and examines their expectations and perceptions in the sociopolitical context of their respective countries, relating these to educational and curricular reforms in each country.

ESL, EFL, and Bilingual Education: Exploring Historical, Sociocultural, Linguistic, and Instructional Foundations, pp. 121–140
Copyright © 2010 by Information Age Publishing
All rights of reproduction in any form reserved.

The purpose of this project was to look at how the changes in society and education are reflected in shifts in the participants' consciousness of themselves as future educators. According to Shea (1996),

> One of the problems of living in a period of transition comes from the disso-
> nance created by an episodic shift away from older meaning systems and our
> inability to react with any kind of sensibility or coherence to the fragmentary
> new symbol systems that strike our bewildered consciousness (p. 40).

The project seeks to answer such questions as: How have changes in the sociopolitical context affected the respondents' perception of themselves as future teachers? How have teaching methodologies shifted? How and why do the participants think these changes have occurred?

REVIEW OF THE LITERATURE/THEORETICAL BACKGROUND

In the past 15 years there have been significant changes is the sociopolitical landscape of Latvia and Poland as they came out of Soviet domination.
Both countries have adopted a democratic political system and are transi-
tioning to a market economy (Bollag, 1999; Kwiek, 2001; Pachocinski,
1997; Soros Foundation, 2001). These changes have brought about shifts
in the philosophies of education in both countries, and created a subsequent need for changes in their educational systems. In the former Soviet
system, conformance was paramount, and the educational systems in for-
merly Soviet-dominated countries reflected this philosophy through an
essentialist and teacher-dominated curriculum (Shipler, 1989). On the
practical level, the political and economic shift in both countries has
decreased the need for vocational education to train workers for industry,
and brought about a need for more academic education to teach citizens
how to live in a democratic society and how to work in a more service-
directed economy (Bollag, 1999; Hamot, 1998; Kwiek, 2001; Pachocinski,
1997; Soros Foundation, 2001; Zachariev, 1999). There is also the need
for people in these countries to have the knowledge and skills needed to
participate in a unified Europe (Kwiek, 2001; Scott, 2002; Snoek et al.,
2003). Philosophically, there has been a shift away

> from the narrow and instrumental role that education played under the pre-
> vious system to a role that is meant to promote social, political, cultural, and
> vocational competencies that are necessary for the individual to carry on a
> successful life individually, socially, and globally. (Pachocinski, 1997, p. 8)

These changes highlight what Eisner and Vallance (1974) refer to as a
curriculum which has social reconstruction-relevance. This orientation to

curriculum suggests that "individual development and the quality of the social context are interdependent" (Eisner & Vallance, 1974, p.11). In other words, education and curriculum are part of a larger social context. This new focus in Latvia and in Poland has created a need for a shift in curriculum development, moving away from the more essentialist education of the past which focused on learning specific knowledge and skills to a more progressive curriculum which recognizes that learning is dynamic and which focuses on the learner.

One educational shift that has occurred as a result of the end of Soviet domination in Poland and Latvia is that more students are studying English as a foreign language than in previous years (Reichelt, 2005; Zimmerman, 2007). The prevalence of English in economic, technological, and industrial development globally, as well as in academic and scientific research, has created a linguistic environment in which access to knowledge and to power have become equated with knowing English (Crystal, 1997). According to Crystal (1997), "A person is more likely to be in touch with the latest thinking and research in a subject by learning English than by learning any other language" (p. 111).

In Poland and Latvia English is seen as a key to improved contact with the rest of the world, and to better employment opportunities, resulting in educational reforms which acknowledge these changes. As with other types of educational reform, the curriculum for foreign language study is shifting. In the past, the foreign language curriculum was grammar-based. The revised curriculum is based on communicative competency, an approach to language education based on Western models, requiring students to learn formal grammar and vocabulary, but also recognizing the need for improved communication skills, using everyday language, and focusing on fluency.

The Polish and Latvian participants in this project grew up and were educated during this time of change and transition. Many of them were small children when the transition from communism occurred and they will be teaching students for whom the current way of life is the norm. This study focuses on how they perceive their roles as future teachers and their perception of their relation to the public sphere.

METHOD

This project is based on interpretative narrative research (McQueen & Zimmerman, 2006), a qualitative research method from the social sciences. Narratives are generated by using a preplanned series of broad, open-ended questions on a particular topic, with additional clarifying questions are asked as needed during the process. Such clarification is shaped by early and ongoing analysis, one of the hallmarks of qualitative research (American Educational Research Association, 2006). The narratives are analyzed by identifying patterns and themes within and among them. The narratives and their analyses are compared with one another and with existing literature on the topic under study (Casey, 1993). Responses are coded using thematic categories which are generated from the language of the respondents.

Unlike quantitative research, and some types of qualitative research, the primary purpose of interpretive narrative research method is to examine an issue situated in a particular context in a particular way. Therefore, this method is not appropriate for every research project, especially those requiring large amounts of data from large samples of people. The researcher chose an adaptation of interpretive narrative method for this project, because the purpose of the project was to investigate a specific research population, seeking specific kinds of information.

Participants

The participants were university students at the English studies department at major universities in Latvia and Poland. All of the respondents were enrolled in the English teaching program at their respective schools. The researcher had met with instructors at each university during summer 2005, and one at each university agreed to ask their students to volunteer for the project. Each instructor was given a packet containing consent forms, a data sheet for contact information, and survey materials. The participants were instructed to return the contact information sheet and the demographic survey to their instructor to mail in a packet to the researcher. Respondents were given the option of completing the surveys and returning them to their instructor to mail in the packet to the researcher, or to email the responses directly to the researcher.

A total of 39 respondents from Poland and 10 respondents from Latvia made up the original sample. Participants responded in written English via mail and email to the survey questions. However, for a variety of reasons, such as no consent form returned, incomplete data, or statements by several respondents that they do not plan to teach, the sample size was reduced. In the end, the researcher analyzed the responses from 9 Latvian and 10 Polish participants.

All of the respondents were scheduled to graduate in spring 2007. All of the Latvian respondents were females in their early 20s. None had taught formally yet. Of the 10 Polish respondents, 2 were male and 8 were female. Seven were in their early 20s, while 2 female respondents were in their late 20s and 1 female respondent was in her mid-40s. Seven of the

Table 10.1. Demographics

Country of Origin	Male	Female	Age (20s)	Age (40s)	Teaching Experience	English Teaching Experience
Latvia		9	9			
Poland	2	8	9	1	7	3

Polish respondents reported having already been teachers, although the three older women were the only ones who reported formal English teaching experiences. One had been teaching for 10 years at the secondary level, another 4 years at the middle school level, and one 6 years at a private school where she taught all ages (see Table 10.1).

Design

This project used demographic and narrative surveys to gather data during Fall 2005 from pre-service English teachers from Poland and Latvia. The demographic survey provided demographic information about the participants, as well as about their current status, and future plans as teachers. The narrative survey consisted of seven questions designed to elicit their expectations and perceptions of themselves as future teachers. The questions were:

1. Why did you decide to be a teacher?
2. Describe your strengths and weaknesses, and how they will impact you as a teacher.
3a. 3a. What is your philosophy of education?
3b. 3b. How has this been shaped by your personal beliefs and values?
4a. 4a. What changes have you seen in education since you were a student?
4b. 4b. How will these differences affect you as a teacher?
5. What impact do governmental policies have on teaching?

Data Analysis

In order to determine where similarities and differences lie between pre-service teachers in the two countries, the narratives were compared with one another within the countries; across countries; and with existing literature on the topic. The analysis focused on these aspects of the responses: the respondents' perceptions and expectations of teaching as a profession; how they view the intersection of the social, political, and educational contexts in their respective countries; and the particular effects they identify as a result of education reforms.

As stated earlier, a few of the participants have already been teachers and are formalizing their education, but most are traditional college students with little or no teaching experience. In analyzing the data, the researcher assumed that this lack of teaching experience would affect the participants' responses. In the preliminary analysis of the preservice teachers' responses, this assumption seems to have been confirmed. Many of the respondents focused primarily on the intrinsic and extrinsic factors which informed their own personal motivations and anxieties about teaching. In general, they seem to have little or no concept of education in the larger sociopolitical arena. After this preliminary analysis, which focused on the personal motivations expressed by the respondents, the narratives were grouped and regrouped to determine patterns which made up the primary thematic categories: needs of society; educational philosophy issues; social changes and impact on education; role of government in education. Each of these categories yielded several subcategories.

Needs of Society

Of the 19 respondents, only one indicated that he had chosen to become a teacher specifically "to help young people become educated and knowledgeable members of society." Another Polish respondent mentioned wanting to help students become successful members of society, but it was not her primary reason for becoming an English teacher.

> As a child I didn't dream about becoming a teacher of English. However, since I remember I adored learning this language.... Time passed and this desire to be a teacher evolved ... I started to love teaching English! Why? It is wonderful to see the happy faces of my students while entering the classroom. It is uplifting to see them engaged in the process of learning during every 45 minutes of each lesson. I know that I can help them to notice the new horizons, to broaden their knowledge and to become the citizens of the United Europe—they will manage to survive because they know English.

In her narrative, she is acknowledging the need that students in her society have for acquiring English, while recognizing her own personal motivations for pursuing the profession.

The rest of the respondents had made the decision to teach English for a variety of reasons. Several indicated that they had originally begun in the program at the university only in order to learn or improve their English. According to Reichelt (2005) many people in Latvia and Poland who study English, even English pedagogy, do not enter the teaching profession, because knowledge of English can lead to better employment opportunities in the business world. This respondent from Poland supports this notion. Because of "the emphasis that they put on practical knowledge of English rather then [*sic*] e.g. English literature," English pedagogy departments often offer an effective way to learn the language. One respondent from Latvia expressed it this way:

> My becoming a teacher was more a matter of a chance—I entered the Faculty of Pedagogy and Psychology after the secondary school to study English because I was interested in this language. Then, step by step, I became aware of the fact that I am really fond of this idea about being a teacher. After getting to know about my teaching in school I decided to go to work there.

One of the Polish women said about her decision to teach:

> It wasn't a deliberate and conscious decision at first. When I took the entry exam … I didn't care so much about the "teacher training" part, I simply wanted to master my English. In the first two years of my studies I didn't even give private lessons. Then I had my first apprenticeship and it turned out to be a very rewarding experience. My students appreciated my patience and the ability to explain everything clearly, some of them even asked me if I could teach them out of school. Then I realized how natural it was for me to pass on my knowledge.

Four of the Latvian respondents said that they selected teaching as a profession because they wanted to work with children and liked the idea of working in the education profession. The Polish respondents answered a little differently, but still focused on personal motivations. Several mentioned the personal satisfaction that teaching as a profession can bring, while one said: "Well, the main reason for my decision was an old family tradition. All women among my relatives are teachers. ;-)" Another mentioned that her French teacher had been a role model. Finally, several mentioned the practical aspects of teaching as a profession, such as having summers off. Overall, most of the participants said they chose to teach out of motivations unrelated to a desire to serve the greater needs of the society.

Educational Philosophy Issues

When the students from Latvia talked about their philosophy of educa-tion and how it would impact them as teachers, their answers reflected three aspects of educational philosophy: development of students as a whole person; education as a lifelong process; and the student-teacher relationship.

One respondent stated that she was a Christian and that this shaped her philosophy of life in general as well as her view of education:

> The holistic approach of the human being, taking into account both its body and soul, is what I stand for. Education should promote the true develop-ment of the person in all the aspects, not only skills and competences (which of course are important), but also conscience, character education and mental values (true, beauty and good) claim the attention. I strongly believe, that this is xtremely [sic] important in the society of the new tech-nologies and information.... Humans are reasonable beings, having con-science and free will. They need other human beings and culture for their development.

Several talked about the value of education and how the educational process shapes their view of life and of education. "Education is a neces-sary process, which helps a person to establish himself in the society and in his own inner world' and another said that "There is no future without education." Two of the respondents mentioned education as a lifelong process. One participant said:

> As I am only in the beginning of my career as a teacher I cannot say much about my philosophy of education because it is changing all the time ... I am not only a young teacher, but a young person as well, and my values are still mutable.

Two of the respondents focused on the teacher-student relationship. One stated that "I try to be equally strict and friendly with all my pupils because, I believe, this is what helps to establish healthy 'teacher—pupil' relationship." Another said that "To teach my pupils and study myself. I belve [sic] that my place is at school with pupils, when they need my help and my advice I am happy."

One Polish respondent said:

> Learning is like a chain, so I tell my students I will keep on learning until I die, and so will they, probably. The most important thing is not to think about your deficiencies, but about the things you know you are good at and need to develop.... Learning a language is a long-term process, it can't be realized overnight.

However, in general, the Polish respondents expressed their philosophies of education differently than the Latvian respondents. They focused more on the needs of the students in two primary ways: practical applications of education to prepare students for their futures, and their role as teachers to facilitate students' acquisition of knowledge. One respondent summed up this view of educational philosophy in this way: "Education should be the base and the rest should be discovered by us."

The Polish respondents seemed very focused on the practical aspects of education. One said, in relation to her own education as an English teacher as well as to her future students,

> I think that education should prepare as to the real life in future, teach us practical not theoretical knowledge that is connected to our field of study. Education should also teach us how to study, help us discover our strong points, preferred learning styles.

Another talked about the need for being prepared for life in the modern world, again referring to her own education as an English teacher and what she should focus on with her students. She said that education should

> be up to date, modern, inventive, and move with the spirit of the time. In my point of view, our profession should change along with the forthcoming trends, should favour the person of the learner and help him develop his own strategies prompting learning in general. It involves new technology as well and it stresses the importance of humanistic teaching and philosophy.

One of the two male respondents echoed this need for practical application of education, by summing up his philosophy of education in this way:

> teaching only these things that will be useful in the future. Only subjects related to prospective specialization, job etc. Lots of people complain about system, which includes subjects that are either unnecessary or they're too long in curriculum of given school.

Besides these practical applications, some of the Polish respondents also talked about how education should prepare students for the future by helping them become active learners. The other male respondent expressed his views this way:

> To help young people understand that it's not just about wisdom or/and knowledge but most of all to help then and teachn [*sic*] them how to think, make good decision and gain more and more useful information for themselves in the process of learning and studing [*sic*].

Some of the participants also talked about how education should be a process of discovery for their students. "To educate means not to teach your students but to help them discover the language on their own, to experiment and play with the information they gather." One felt that her students should not only discover practical knowledge, but knowledge which would help them to be better people. "Education is for me helping people to reach higher state of mind and spirit. Shearing [*sic*] vital knowledge that allows students to achieve personal goals to be better person is the key of my personal philosophy of education."

Another respondent who has been teaching for several years expressed this same desire to facilitate students' learning:

> The role of the teacher should not involve the transition of knowledge but mainly facilitation of students' knowledge in the follow up process of education and motivating them to discover knowledge themselves. The role of the teacher that I find the most important should be to increase students' confidence and self-esteem. Polish students have incredibly low self-esteem and they do not believe in themselves.... Appreciate their individuality and autonomy and use it to facilitate the process of gaining knowledge.

Several of the respondents made direct connections to the way that they were taught and the way that they teach now. One who has been teaching for several years said:

> the way I teach is not the reflection of how I myself was taught. I had negative attitude towards education in general. A teacher's role was mainly of an instructor and controller. My attitude has changed a lot since I learned how to teach and manage teaching processes in the classroom. I mastered some techniques and methods which I try to implement. I know what works best because I have established some teaching strategies over a period of time. This I believe shapes me as a teacher and gives pleasure while teaching.

Another participant who had been teaching for several years summed up her progressive, student-centered philosophy of education in this way:

> I think education system should be adjusted to learners. A teacher should understand that his subject is not the most important one and therefore should understand learners who do not feel like learning it. It does not mean a teacher should let a learner do what he wants and not to learn at all. However, a teacher should be aware of learner's preferences, type of intelligence [*sic*], etc. My philosophy of education is to show learners that language learning is a fun but also hard and rewarding work.

Social Changes' Impact on Education

Two of the questions (4a and 4b) focused on how the respondents viewed educational changes in their societies and how they perceived it would affect them as teachers. Many of the responses from participants in both countries focused on the increased freedom of teachers and students, as well as changes in the amount of authority teachers have and the amount of responsibility that students feel they have. One respondent commented that education "has become more student-centered and autonomous. I am not the only source of knowledge but responsible for teaching students how to learn."

Two of the Latvian respondents stated that they did not see any changes in education in their lifetimes, although one did state that teachers have more autonomy now to make decisions about what they teach. Another Latvian respondent agreed that this increased autonomy was a positive change. The other Latvian respondents stated that along with this increased freedom and autonomy for teachers was a concurrent freedom for students that they did not see as always positive. One respondent summed it up this way: "Teachers used to be more respected."

Several respondents said that students have less of a sense of responsibility for their own learning and there are more discipline problems in the classes. One addressed the issue of reforms, and how she saw them as creating more work for teachers.

> There have been many changes in the National Curriculum especially in the last few years which strongly influence teachers' work. Pupils can be divided in two different categories: highly motivated and totally unmotivated ones. Teachers have to think of different methods to make lessons more interesting for both categories of pupils, as well as cover the necessary material for the National Curriculum.

The Polish respondents answered these questions at more length than did the Latvians. Their answers tended to fall into three categories: the re-structuring of Polish schools; new teaching methods; and lack of respect for teachers by students. One respondent who has already been teaching for 6 years said there has been a general "loss of satisfaction in teaching." She went on to say that "Teachers no longer educate, they produce students. Students are not human beings they are commodities. This is dilemma in capitalistic Western countries where possessing goods most is appreciated rather than being a better person."

One of the major reforms that Polish education underwent during the early 2000s, was to restructure the schools from a K-8, 9-12 format to a K-6, 7-9, 10-12 format (I am using nomenclature from the U.S. system).

Several respondents commented on the effects of this change, and most agree that this change was not for the better. One respondent said:

> The changes in the structure of education, especially the existence of lower secondary school [junior high] makes teacher's work more difficult especially in terms of discipline. It is well-known that this age is quite difficult for teenagers. Nowadays, many people wonder if it was a good idea to put all those kids in one place. I've never thought [sic] in lower secondary school, my friend who teaches there told me that this is the worse place for the teacher to teach. A lot of kids don't care about school and they make teacher's life horrible.

One Polish participant spoke directly to reforms as they related to foreign language teaching, particularly English teaching.

> The structure of English teaching curriculum has changed over the last years for the better, I hope. I stared learning English at my own request when I was 9 years old, but it wasn't obligatory at the primary school until the fifth grade. Apart from that there was no continuity between the primary and secondary school, students were at different levels, so year one was merely a revision [in American English—review] for half a group and pretty hard work to catch up for the rest. Now, teaching foreign languages starts from the first grade, and there is a competence test after each level of education, for example, primary school, then after graduating from "gimnazjum" [junior high], and the results are the base for applying into higer [sic] level schools.

Many of the Polish respondents referred to their own experiences in school as they described changes in methods, strategies and techniques that they are learning in their English teacher training courses. One of the participants spoke about the changing role of a teacher and their responsibilities toward their students.

> Definitely, there is much more interest in the learner himself. All the exercises tend to be contextualized and they move on according to topics. The teacher is not the one and only authority punishing poor students with bad grades but he is supposed to be a helper, mental health worker, learner and not only controller and organizer.

One of the male respondents commented about the change in the teacher's role, and the change toward more practical and relevant materials and information.

> When I was a student there was mostly just unusful [sic] information and knowledge taught at school, in most topics just encyclopedical [sic] information. Now it is changing, to give students more practical preparation in the

modern. Now is really more easy to teach when you can do more things that in the past were impossible. I have more freedom in what I do with young people and how I do it. It's very important not just to be a teacher but also give them example and this is now also more possible e.g. to become not a teacher/superviser [*sic*] but almost a friend, someone who helps them open new doors of opportunities [*sic*].

One of the respondents mentioned her own education as a pre-service teacher, as well as her own English learning experiences. She also went on to talk about other changes that she thinks have an impact on students in Polish schools.

The greatest gap I have noticed in teaching was that between the theory of teaching I learnt at the Teacher Training College and the real life experiences I had from school as a student. Nobody had taught me English this way, ever. And also there is a new "matura" examination after the secondary school, new procedures and expectations of students' skills and knowledge, this you can simply learn from the ministry website or the school authorities. Not to mention the vast numbers of books available on the market, there used to be one set of books handed over from older siblings or cousins, now the variety makes you feel dizzy when you get into a bookstore, and of course each teacher in every school prefers one particular coursebook to another.

Role of Government in Education

Two respondents, one from Poland and one from Latvia said they were not aware of how government policies affect education, and three of the respondents from Latvia gave very general answers to the question of how government policies affect education. One respondent from each country mentioned low salaries for teachers as an important governmental issue. Three respondents from each country focused on curricular changes.

One of the Polish respondents said that "The government gives us a lot of freedom. Teachers chose materials and teaching styles. The government only imposes program's minimum." Another commented that teachers have "some kind of freedom like in type of materials to use but still there are some expactation [*sic*] and demands on teacher." A third respondent from Poland stated: "The only intervention are probably the key competences [*sic*] we have to realize during each lesson but the rest of the material tends to be up to us—teachers."

Two of the Latvian respondents made general comments about government's role in curriculum decisions, but one respondent from Latvia commented that even though curricular changes were the most obvious, she has "a feeling that also fre [*sic*] market and lobby play significant role in education." Although she did not elaborate on this statement, it is obvious that she sees that the situation is more complex than mere change to curriculum. Another respondent from Latvia commented on the confusion that teachers often feel due to these curricular changes. She mentioned the specific changes that have come about in the English curriculum and how it has created problems for teachers.

> Introduction of English exam on the state level has divided teachers in two parts—those supporting the exam and those being against it. This is another state policy towards educational system that needs a lot of explanations on teachers and school authorities' level.

The Polish participants had more to say on this issue than the Latvian participants did. Several focused on financial policy, not just teacher salaries, but how financial policies affect teachers and student in other ways. One of the Polish respondents explained it this way:

> Low salaries, not enough money for schooling result in the lack of good teachers, discrimination of poorer students whose parents cannot afford to buy expensive books, lack of appropriate institutions for students with specific problems such as ADHD and appropriate teachers to teach them.

Another lamented the financial constraints that education is under, and how it engenders a lack of respect for the professionalism of the field:

> The money the government spends on education has never sufficed the financial needs of any school in Poland. The subsidies for education are so poor that in many schools there is not enough money to buy even chalk, not to mention things like teaching aids or electronic equipment like overhead projectors or computers. More and more often teachers themselves look for sponsors to found the most basic teaching aids. This situation has rather negative impact on teaching because it does not make teaching professional.

One of the male students from Poland also addressed how government fiscal policy is affecting college students, even those who want to become teachers:

> Government wants students to pay for studies both at state and private colleges. Students should also have higher financial resources. There's also a system of scholarships and credits which is meant to be introduced to help students became financially independent from their parents. (taken from http://serwisy.gazeta.pl/edukacja/1,51805,2851446.html)

Several of the Polish respondents also commented on specific reforms that had taken place in Poland in the last few years. One of the changes in Polish in the education in the last few years has been a change in the structure of the schools, as described earlier. One participant described the new system and described the changes brought about by reform as "Major." Another respondent, a woman who has been teaching for several years described what she sees as the negative effects of the change from a middle school environment (U.S. Grades 6-8) to a junior high environment (U.S. Grade 7-9).

> I teach in *gimnazjum* where learners' age is from 13 to 16. They are all gathered in the same school which is new in our Polish education system and not necessarily beneficial. We have problems with these schools. Additionally, children at this age undergo different mental and physical changes and it is difficult for a teacher to cope with many problems.

Another respondent spoke about the reforms and focused on how the they impacted foreign language education in particular.

> As far as foreign languages are concerned there has been much changed in the field of communicative purpose—nowadays the stress is put on the communication itself. It is very important, we—the members of the European Union, will have much more opportunities to visit foreign countries and to communicate.

DISCUSSION

The responses of most of the participants support what the literature has said regarding the philosophical shift in education in their respective countries post-communism. Most of them agree that education reforms were necessary to meet the needs of modern society. Most of the participants also recognized the role that government policies play in shaping education, although some had a clearer vision of how these policies actually play out in the educational setting than others. A few respondents also discussed the confusion that teachers often experience as a result of reforms. Several spoke of the philosophical issues related to the changes, which have moved the educational system toward more progressive, student-centered learning. While some spoke of the greater freedom that teachers and students have to direct the learning, a few felt that students have too much freedom, which translates into less responsibility for the students and less authority for the teacher.

According to Shea (1996), there is dissonance between old and new when changes are made. In both countries, the teacher candidates are being taught a new orientation to curriculum based on education reforms. Some of them embrace these new ways of teaching and others seem to resist it. In the narratives, dissonance is demonstrated as slippage between what the respondents say about the new methods and strategies of education, and their perceptions of how these reforms are affecting education. These slippages manifested themselves as tensions in the participants' perspectives, and even as contradictions at times. Examining these slippages highlights how curriculum is taken for granted by educators, even potential educators, and how curricular reform can often be seen by educators as unnecessary, ill-conceived, or irrelevant.

Slippages were most apparent in the narratives of the Polish respondents. On one hand, many of them talked favorably about the new student-centered focus of education, and the increased amount of autonomy teachers have for selecting strategies and materials. However, they also expressed concern about the lack of responsibility that students seem to exhibit for their learning, and how respect for teachers and their authority has decreased. The respondents seem to perceive that this freedom results in a loss of authority.

Several questions arise from this slippage. Are they trying to reconcile their own education, in the prereform days with what they are learning in their current teacher education program? How effective are their teacher education programs in helping them make the transition from their own experiences? According to Doll (1988), in his analysis of educational practice in the United States in the 1980s, curriculum and teaching are a process, in which the educator creates "knowledge of how one works in practice, not just applying knowledge that others have generalized and formalized" (p. 119). However he goes on to say that "current professional training does not encourage the practitioner to look—intuitively, metaphorically, personally—at the situation at hand; nor to reflect on the actions in process, changing ends and means in midstream; nor to search for anomalies in analysis" (p. 119).

Doll's (1988) analysis raises further questions about the respondents' perceptions of teacher and student behavior. Are classes really more student-centered, or are teachers trying to fit different methods and strategies into their traditional ways of teaching, causing students to misunderstand the goals of the lessons and resist participating appropriately? Are students being irresponsible or are the participants perceiving the "controlled chaos" of a student-centered classroom as disrespect, lack of responsibility, and lack of control, because they do not really understand or accept this way of teaching?

When we consider that the participants are training to be English teachers, we should also consider the impact of what Yukio Tsuda calls the "Diffusion of English Paradigm"(Phillipson & Skutnabb-Kangas, 1997). Tsuda contends that the English Paradigm is based in part in capitalism, modernization through technology and globalization, and "Americanization and homogenization of world culture" (Phillipson & Skutnabb-

Kangas, 1997, p. 39). It is important to consider that English is not only being taught as a language, but forms part of the canon of globalization. It is relevant to question whether philosophies of education modeled on the "English-speaking world" (Phillipson & Skutnabb-Kangas, 1997) are appropriate and relevant for post-communist countries such as Poland and Latvia.

For example, in Shea's (1996) discussion of education in the postmodern world, she favors constructive ecological postmodernism, which "places the person on a continuum where an awareness of past and future generations helps to define what constitutes meaningful knowledge, values, and responsibility" (p. 46). She thinks that "our communities and schools can become an important part of the transformation toward more sustainable, human-scale, postmodern communities" (p. 36). How are these ideas relevant to post-Communist Poland and Latvia? Although their governments and societies are trying to emulate the Western democracies and are embracing the economic power of capitalism, have they followed the same philosophical trajectory as the "western" world or has their past created a different track? How does knowledge of English constitute and contribute to what Shea (1996) refers to as "meaningful knowledge, values, and responsibility" (p. 46) for post-Communist Poland and Latvia? These and other similar questions can be used to guide further research on these issues.

IMPLICATIONS FOR FURTHER STUDY

This pilot study has shown that some methodological changes should be implemented before continuing the project. These include changes to how the responses are elicited; changes in the focus of the questions; and changes in the participant pool.

Several changes to the survey design and the implementation of the surveys would provide more in-depth responses from participants. The length and quality of the respondents' answers may have been affected because the surveys were administered in English rather than in their home language. Conducting interviews with the participants as well as their filling out surveys would give the researcher and participant more flexibility for clarification and elaboration.

The original group of questions focused more on education in general and not on English teaching specifically. Although most of the participants did frame their responses in the context of themselves as future English teachers, questions more to the point of their role as English teachers would have elicited specific answers about how they perceive the role of English in their society.

Changing the participant pool would also affect the results. The next planned phase of this project is to collect data from in-service English teachers and compare their responses to that of these pre-service teachers. Practitioners in the field will have different perspectives on educational reform since they will have taught in both systems, and during the transition. Including preservice teachers and in-service from fields besides English might offer different perspectives on the issues facing teachers in the respective countries. Data from teachers already in the field and from teacher educators and administrators at the college and university levels give more depth and breadth to the ideas presented here. It would also be enlightening to talk to policymakers about the decisions that have been made about education in these countries as well as to where reforms may be headed.

CONCLUSION

Although political and economic change in former Soviet-Bloc countries brought hope for the future, it also brought the realization that the existing educational system would not prepare citizens of these countries for the future in the global economy, and in a unified Europe. The reforms in the foreign language curriculum, and the shift to a greater emphasis on teaching English, is a direct result of these changes. Although English is not the "official" language of the European Union (Europa, 2006), much of its business is conducted in English. According to Knight.eu (n.d.), "the expansion of the European Union and of English as a commercial language have gone hand in hand, and consequently there is great demand for instruction, both in the education sector and in the private sector" (para. 10). The experiences of these university students who have lived during the time of the transitions shed some light on the effect that the reforms are having on education in Poland and in Latvia. Their experiences reflect the tensions and ambiguity inherent in societal and subsequent educational and curricular change. It is not always possible to say at what point a change happens or must happen. Just as many of these respondents evolved into English teachers, so educational reform must evolve and change with conditions. Since we cannot predict the future, educational reform must address the issues that exist in the present, and remain flexible enough to be relevant in a variety of futures.

REFERENCES

American Educational Research Association. (2006). Standards for reporting on empirical social science research in AERA Publications. *Educational Researcher, 35*(6), 33-40.

Bollag, B. (1999). Reforms in higher education disappoint Eastern Europeans. *Chronicle of Higher Education, 46*(5), A55-A56.

Casey, K. (1993). *I answer with my life: Life histories of women teachers working for social change*. New York: Routledge.

Crystal, D. (1997). *English as a global language* (2nd ed.) Cambridge, England: Cambridge University Press.

Doll, W. (1988). Curriculum beyond stability: Schon, Prigogine, Piaget. In W. Pinar (Ed.), *Contemporary curriculum discourses* (pp. 114-133). Scottsdale, AZ: Gorsuch Searsbrick.

Eisner, E., & Vallance, E. (Eds.). (1974). Five conceptions of curriculum: Their roots and implications for curriculum planning. In *Conflicting conceptions of curriculum* (pp. 1-18). Berkley, CA: McCutchan.

Europa. (2006). *Welcome to the Europa languages portal!* Retrieved September 27, 2006 from http://europa.eu/languages/en/home

Hamot, G. (1998). A case of teacher education reform in Poland's transitional democracy. *European Education, 30*(2), 5-24.

Knight.eu. (n.d.). Teaching English as a foreign language. *Knight.eu: Teaching English as a foreign language: A European informational website*. Retrieved from http://www.knight.eu/teaching_english_as_a_foreign_language_en.html

Kwiek, M. (2001). Social and cultural dimensions of the transformation of higher education in Central and Eastern Europe. *Higher Education in Europe, 26*(3), 399-410.

McQueen, L., & Zimmerman, L. (2006). Using interpretive narrative research methodology in interdisciplinary research projects: Issues in the education of Hispanic nurses. *Journal of Nursing Education, 45*(11), 475-478.

Pachocinski, R. (1997). Educational Development in Central and Eastern Europe. *European Education, 29*(3), 6-25.

Phillipson, R., & Skutnabb-Kangas, T. (1997). Linguistic human rights and English in Europe. *World Englishes, 16*(1), 27-43.

Reichelt, M. (2005). English in Poland, *World Englishes, 24*(2), 217-225.

Scott, P. (2002). Reflections on the reform of higher education in Central and Eastern Europe. *Higher Education in Europe, 27*(1-2), 137-152.

Shea, C. (1996). Critical and constructive postmodernism: The transformative power of holistic education. *Holistic Education Review, 9*(3), 40-49.

Shipler, D. (1989). *Russia: Broken idols, solemn dreams*. New York, NY: Times Books.

Snoek, M., Fino, C., Halstead, V., Hilton, G., Mikl, J., Rehn, J., et al. (2003). Reflections on trends in teacher education in Europe using the scenario perspective. *European Journal of Teacher Education, 26*(1), 137-142.

Soros Foundation—Latvia. (2001). *A passport to social cohesion and economic prosperity: Report of education in Latvia 2000*. Riga, Latvia: Author.

Zachariev, Z. (1999). Recent developments in education in Central and Eastern Europe. *European Education, 31*(3), 25-39.

Zimmerman, L. (2007). Reflections on standard English in the EFL classroom. *ELT Journal, 61*(2), 164-166.

REFLECTION QUESTIONS

1. What factors contribute to some of the differences in the students' responses in the two countries?
2. How would teachers in your country respond to similar questions about education in your country?
3. What is relationship between society and education?

FOLLOW-UP ACTIVITIES

1. Interview a teacher about the effects of educational reform in your country.
2. Create a timeline of education and educational reform in your country which also shows key societal, economic, political, etc. events.

FURTHER READING

- Crystal, D. (2003). *English as a global language,* (2nd ed.). Cambridge, England: Cambridge University Press.
- Kaplan, A. (1994). *French lessons: A memoir.* Chicago, IL: University of Chicago Press.

CHAPTER 11

TEACHING BILINGUAL STUDENTS WITH SPECIAL NEEDS

A Teacher Training Issue

INTRODUCTION

In general, English as a Second Language (ESL), bilingual education, and general classroom teachers are inadequately prepared to work with English Language Learners (ELLs) who have special needs. This chapter is an overview of research literature which examines educational, administrative, community, and policy surrounding this topic in order to determine how schools of education can better prepare teachers to work with this population of students.

This issue of special needs and the English Language Learner is a complex and complicated one. It involves all of the issues that education for children with special needs has, such as legal issues, psychological issues, parental involvement issues, and the involvement of general education classroom teachers. These issues are intertwined with those of the English Language Learner, such as limited English proficiency of the child and/or parent, cultural issues, language learning issues, and the ability of general education to adequately meet the needs of the ELL students. The

ESL, EFL, and Bilingual Education: Exploring Historical, Sociocultural, Linguistic, and Instructional Foundations, pp. 141–148
Copyright © 2010 by Information Age Publishing
All rights of reproduction in any form reserved.

research reviewed here shows that teachers need more specialized training in order to work more effectively with these students.

AN OVERVIEW OF THE RESEARCH

Teacher Efficacy

A study by Paneque and Barbetta (2006) correlate teaching ELLs with
special needs and teacher efficacy. They asserted that teachers, whether
general education or special education, with high efficacy believe they can
positively affect student learning and will make an effort to do so. They
also found that teachers with high efficacy tend to make fewer special
education referrals. When they examined efficacy as related to ELLs, they
found that, by and large, general education and special education teachers, even those with high efficacy, feel least efficacious with ELL students.
They cited teacher issues and organizational issues as coming into play.
Teacher issues that they identified included dispositions and attitudes,
teaching skills, preparation, experience, and field-based experiences in
teacher education programs. Organizational issues included language
support, and parental support.

An earlier study by Brownell and Parajes (1996, 1999) had found that
training is important in building teacher efficacy, whether preservice
teacher training or in-service training. The study by Paneque and Barbetta (2006) supports this finding. They stated "that there was need for
professional training in issues related to the education of culturally and
linguistically diverse students with disabilities for individuals working with
those students" (p. 186).

Language Training

One of the issues that Paneque and Barbetta (2006) focused on was
that teachers should have knowledge of the student's home language, and
they advocate language training for preservice and in-service teachers of
students with special needs. Citing work by other researchers, who had
examined issue in the assessment and instruction of bilingual students
with special needs (Artiles & Ortiz, 2002; Baca & Cervantes, 2004; Delgado & Rogers-Adkinson, 1999; Winzer & Mazurek, 1998), Paneque and
Barbetta (2006) stated that "these experts assert that the use of native language instruction and the development of the native language allow ELLs
to build on their prior knowledge and support learning new content
material" (p. 184). They also cite work by Carlson, Brauen, Klein,

Schrool, and Willig (2002) which "found that special education teachers proficient in the language of their students were able to use different instructional strategies to teach English language and academic content" (p. 184). Besides helping the students communicate and learn better in the classroom, Paneque and Barbetta (2006) also asserted that knowledge of the students' home language facilitates communication with parents.

This research is supported by Mueller, Singer, and Grace (2004) who determined that there is no research on how ELL students with learning difficulties are affected by trying to learn two languages—their home language and English. However, the authors have surmised from research by Cummins (1991) and Donovan and Cross (2002) that students with such disabilities need to learn to communicate effectively in their home language before trying to learn another language. Their reasoning is that "children identified as having moderate or severe disabilities typically display many difficulties with communication and language acquisition" (p. 232).

Policy Issues

The Mueller et al. (2004) study found that policy issues and administrative decisions affect the teachers' ability to work with ELL students with disabilities effectively. When policies are ambiguous, school practices tend to be inconsistent and the teachers in this study "reported that their administration did not provide the teachers with guidance regarding planning, assessment, or instructional practices for the ELL students in their classrooms" (p. 243). The researchers recognized such inconsistency as being a serious problem "because children with disabilities are so dependent upon appropriate language and communication programs, it is even more crucial that ELLs with disabilities are provided with well-thought-out and well-developed language instruction" (p. 237). Therefore, they emphasize the importance of teachers receiving proper training in how to work with ELL students. The teachers in this study also expressed an interest in learning Spanish, so they could communicate better with their Spanish-speaking students and their families.

Parental Support

Robinson's (2000) research found that if schools set up effective support for parents, the teacher will be able to more effectively teach ELLs with special needs. She emphasized that parents of ELL children with disabilities do want to be involved with their children's education but often obstacles such as not speaking English, or not speaking it well, their own limited experience with schooling, lack of time, and general lack of information about what services are available and how to attain them stand in the way. Oftentimes these parents do not know what their rights are, and may assume the school is doing the best thing for their child. Robinson (2000) states that the educator must be aware that there are different cultural norms for how one interacts with school personnel and differing cultural views of special needs.

In their examination of special education services for ELLs, Torres-Burgo, Reyes-Wasson, and Brusca-Vega (1999) found that ELL students with special needs are often misdiagnosed and do not receive adequate proper services. Like Robinson (2000) they assert that part of the problem is that parents who do not know English or have limited English often do not have adequate access to information about their child with special needs—what their rights are and what services are available. According to research by Torres-Burgo et al. (1999), despite regulations in IDEA (Individuals with Disabilities Education Act) which are supposed to guarantee parental access and involvement, non-English speaking parents students actually receive less information and clarification than English speaking parents. The research also found that in order for parental support programs to be effective, school administration has to be supportive.

Hoover and Patton (2005) also suggest that ELLs often are overidentified, underidentified, and/or misidentified for special education services because "the learning and behavior problems of ELL students may encompass several factors, such as different sociolinguistic and cultural background, adjustment to a new sociocultural milieu, the presence of a disability, or a combination of these factors" (p. 231). This statement supports the findings of Gonzalez, Brusca-Vega, and Yawkey (1997) in their study of assessment and instruction issues related to culturally and linguistically diverse students.

Instructional Issues

Because of the complexity of these students' needs, their instruction must be multifaceted in order to be effective, incorporating a variety of techniques and strategies. Hoover and Patton (2005) assert that "differentiation must take place in the mainstream classroom and the resource room to be most effective" (p. 234). Hoover, Klinger, Baca, and Patton (2008) support using a variety of instructional strategies and practices, including differentiated learning, three-tiered instruction, response to intervention (RTI), and standards-based learning and assessment to effectively teach students who are ELL and have special needs. Chamot and

O'Malley (1994) also assert that effective teaching for ELLs and ELLs with disabilities must focus on content and language as well as on cognitive development. They state that: "Students with learning disabilities represent the largest category of special education students and [benefit] from learning strategy instruction" (p. 180).

Hoover et al. (2008) assert that the special education teacher already has knowledge and expertise about adapting curriculum to meet individual student needs. Teaching ELL students with special needs requires this same type of perspective on teaching with a bit more complexity. "Teachers must become familiar with several interrelated elements of education, including linguistically diverse education, second language acquisition, special education needs and characteristics, and the role of culture in teaching and learning" (p. 5). Therefore, instruction for these students must be appropriate and the curriculum should reflect an understanding of their cultural values (Hoover & Patton, 2005). Hoover et al. (2008) cite research that supports their perspective that the challenges faced by the special needs bilingual student, "a range of cognitive, academic, and language learning needs," (p.89) can best be met with "careful planning and intervention" (p. 89). They also emphasize that education for these students be approached from a strengths-based model which "emphasizes high expectations for these students" (p. 89), rather than from the traditional deficit model which focuses on the students' limitations. Collaboration between the special education staff and the bilingual/ESL staff are essential to provide the best education for this population of students.

Several models of bilingual/ESL Special Education are presented by Hoover et al. (2008). They suggest that in the best of all possible worlds, there would be an integrated model in which there is "a bilingual special education teacher who is trained in both fields and able to deliver the services independently" (p. 91). Unfortunately the model implemented in a school often depends on financial considerations and availability of qualified teachers rather than on needs of the students.

Legal Issues

Hoover et al. (2008) remind their readers that there are also legal issues involved in teaching students with special needs no matter their linguistic background. IDEA 2004 and No Child Left behind (NCLB) both mandate how children with disabilities must be educated, and in different ways, each provides support for accommodations for students with disabilities.

DISCUSSION AND CONCLUSION

The various studies presented here demonstrate the complexity and the variety of the issues when educating ELLs with special needs. Whether the issues are directly related to the teacher, such as assessment and instructional issues, or issues to be dealt with on the larger scale such as policy and administration issues in the school, or legal and parental rights issues in the school community, the teacher is often the person in the best position to be the student's advocate.

Based on the information from these studies, I believe that schools of education should consider a Teaching ESL/Bilingual Students with Special Needs course as a requirement for all ESL and bilingual education majors, and it should be offered as an elective for general education teachers. The issues and needs of these students are different from and more complex than those of ELL students who do not have special needs. There are different demands at all levels, the school, the teacher, the family, and the student. Professional training which directly addresses these issues can help teachers advocate for and facilitate establishing consistent policies at all levels. Whether developing language skills, or learning specific techniques for working with these students, professional development aimed working with English language students with special needs will improve teacher efficacy and help teachers best serve all their students.

REFERENCES

Artiles, A., & Ortiz, A. (Eds.). (2002). English language learners with special education needs: Contexts and possibilities. In *English language learners with special education needs: Identification, assessment, and instruction* (pp. 3-27). McHenry, IL: Center for Applied Linguistics.

Baca, L., & Cervantes, H. (2004). *The bilingual special education interface* (4th ed.). Upper Saddle River, NJ: Prentice-Hall.

Carlson, E., Brauen, M., Klein, S., Schrool, K., & Willig, S. (2002). Study of personnel need in special education. Rockville, MD: Westat Research Corporation. Retrieved June 10, 2008 from http://www.ecs.org/html/offsite.asp?document=http%3A%2F%2Fferdig%2Ecoe%2Eufl%2Eedu%2Fspense%2FKeyFindings%2Epdf+

Chamot, A., & O'Malley, J. (1994). *The CALLA handbook: Implementing the cognitive academic language learning approach*. New York, NY: Addison-Wesley.

Cummins, J. (1991). Interdependence of first- and second-language proficiency in bilingual children. In E. Bialystok (Ed.), *Language processing in bilingual children* (pp. 70-89). Cambridge, England: Cambridge University Press.

Delgado, B., & Rogers-Adkinson, D. (1999). Educating the Hispanic-American exceptional learner. *Advances in Special Education, 12,* 53-71.

Donovan, S., & Cross, C. (Eds.). (2002). *Minority students in special and gifted education.* Washington, DC: National Research Council.

Gonzalez, V., Brusca-Vega, R., & Yawkey, T. (1997) *Assessment and instruction of culturally and linguistically diverse student with or at-risk of learning problems.* Needham Heights, MA: Allyn & Bacon.

Hoover, J., Klinger, J., Baca, L., & Patton, J. (2008). *Methods for teaching culturally and linguistically diverse exceptional learners.* Upper Saddle River, NJ: Pearson.

Hoover, J. & Patton, J. (2005, March). Differentiating curriculum and instruction for English-Language Learners with special needs. *Intervention in School and Clinic, 40*(4), 231-235.

Mueller, T., Singer, G., & Grace, E. (2004, Summer). The Individuals with Disabilities Education Act and California's Proposition 227: Implications for English language learners with special needs. *Bilingual Research Journal, 28*(2), 231-251.

Paneque, O., & Barbetta, P. (2006, Spring). A study of teacher efficacy of special education teachers of English Language Learners with disabilities. *Bilingual Research Journal,* 30(1), 171-193.

Robinson, D. (2000, Summer). Involvement of Portuguese speaking parents in the education of their special-needs children. *Bilingual Research Journal, 24*(3): 309-324.

Torres-Burgo, N., Reyes-Wasson, P., & Brusca-Vega, R. (1999, Fall). Perceptions and needs of Hispanic and non-Hispanic parents of children receiving learning disabilities services. *Bilingual Research Journal, 23*(4), 373-388.

Winzer, M., & Mazurek, K. (1998). *Special education in multicultural contexts.* Upper Saddle River, NJ: Prentice-Hall.

REFLECTION QUESTIONS

1. Why is special education training needed for ESL teachers?
2. What kind of outreach can school do to help parents of students who are ESL with special needs?
3. How can consistent and unambiguous policies help teachers be more effective witht his population of students?

FOLLOW-UP ACTIVITIES

1. Research the various laws that relate to ESL and special education. How do they protect the students' rights? Where do they fall short?
2. Examine the websites and catalogs of 10 major universities in your area that have TESL programs. Do they offer special education courses for their students who are training to be ESL teachers?

FURTHER READING

- Root, C. (1994). A guide to learning disabilities for the ESL classroom practitioner. *TESL-EJ, 1*(1). Retrieved from http://www-writing .berkeley.edu/tesl-ej/ej01/a.4.html
- Whitten, E., Esteves, K., & Woodrow, A. (2009). *RTI success: Proven tools and strategies for schools and classrooms.* Minneapolis, MN: Free Spirit.

PART IV

Effectively Teaching Bilingual/ESL/EFL Students

Should I have a coma in the middle of this sentence?

—From InnocentEnglish.com (n.d.)

Sometimes educators comment that strategies for teaching ESL/EFL students is just good teaching practice. One uses strategies and techniques that would work with any student. While this is true, it is not the entire picture. ESL/EFL students have specific needs that must be addressed because they are learning the language, as well as content, so the teacher must be careful not to take students' language ability for granted. Lessons designed for these students need to have language learning objectives as well as other learning objectives. It is not enough to say, for example, that the student will compare and record the sizes of objects. The teacher must know first of all if the students know how to express comparison in English. Whether they do or not, the lesson for EFL/ESL students should include comparison of adjectives as a language objective.

Although some of the issues are different for ESL students who are immersed in English and EFL students who are learning English mainly in the classroom environment, the stages of language acquisition and the

ESL, EFL, and Bilingual Education: Exploring Historical, Sociocultural, Linguistic, and Instructional Foundations, pp. 149–151
Copyright © 2010 by Information Age Publishing

conditions for optimal learning are similar. Optimal language learning occurs when the language interaction requires the learner to operate slightly above their current state. Vygotsky (Richard-Amato, 2003) explained that learning happens on a continuum with "where the learner is" at one end and "potential development" on the other. The in-between area, he identified as the zone of proximal development (ZPD), the area where the learner can perform above their present ability with assistance in order to move toward independence.

Stephen Krashen (Richard-Amato, 2003) agrees that optimal language learning occurs when the learner operates slightly above their current state, what he terms $i + 1$ (i is the present level and 1 is the next step above). He believes that reading is key to student success and he states that "People who say they read more typically read better and have a more mature writing style" (Krashen, 2004, p. 8). Krashen is a strong proponent of free voluntary reading as a way of improving language skills. He asserts that "in-school free reading programs are consistently effective" (p. 2) for English speakers and for English language learners. Because it is free and voluntary, the student has chosen what they want to read, the activity is less stressful than when readings are assigned and enforced. Krashen's research has shown that lowering the affective filter in this way promotes better reading and literacy. Free reading not only promotes growth in literacy, but improves vocabulary, grammar, spelling, writing, oral/aural language skills, and increases general knowledge.

This final section of the book offers some ideas for how to engage ESL/EFL students in a variety of activities that go beyond the grammar worksheet and vocabulary drill. Because most of the essays in this section are based on workshop presentations, they are present practical strategies and techniques to use in the classroom.

- Chapter 12: "Teaching Abstract Concepts in the EFL Classroom" explains an activity enabling EFL/ESL students to engage in higher level discussions. (Originally published: Zimmerman, L. W. (2005, February). Teaching abstract concepts in the EFL classroom. *The Internet TESL Journal: For Teachers of English as a Second Language* [online], *11*. Available at http://iteslj.org/Lessons/Zimmerman-AbstractConcepts/. Reprinted with permission of the publisher.)

- Chapter 13: "Let Every Voice Be Heard: Creating Effective Groups" presents how to create groups which work effectively in the ESL/EFL classroom.

- Chapter 14: "Using FVR in the ESL Classroom" examines Krashen's notion of free voluntary reading and how it can be implemented effectively in the bilingual/ESL classroom.

- Chapter 15: "The School Library and the ESL Student" is aimed at the school library media specialist, but is useful for teachers to see how they can reasonably expect the librarian to help them and their students.
- Chapter 16: "Teaching About Prejudice Using YouTube and TeacherTube" explains activities that incorporate language skills and teach about a serious topic such as "prejudice" using materials from YouTube and TeacherTube.

REFERENCES

InnocentEnglish.com. (n.d.). Retrieved from http://www.innocentenglish.com/funny-english-mistakes-bloopers/funny-english-student-mistakes/funniest-student-bloopers.html

Krashen, S. (2004). *The power of reading: Insights from the research* (2nd ed.). Portsmouth, NH: Libraries Unlimited.

Richard-Amato, P. (2003). *Making it happen: From interactive to participatory language teaching* (3rd ed.). White Plains, NY: Longman.

CHAPTER 12

TEACHING ABSTRACT CONCEPTS IN THE EFL CLASSROOM

INTRODUCTION

For several summers I have taught English in a 3-week summer camp for Polish high school students who come from all over Poland to improve their spoken English skills with native speakers. One of the challenges of teaching in such a camp is that students want to have fun, and not have dull, repetitive lessons. I successfully used an abstract concept, freedom, to intellectually challenge the students while giving them an opportunity to practice their spoken English at an appropriate skill level.

FRAMING THE CONCEPT

Abstract concepts can be difficult to discuss effectively without preparation and structure. Since I was teaching in Poland, I decided to call on Polish history to help me frame a discussion about "freedom." However, I have found that students often speak more readily about topics which directly concern themselves and their families. Therefore, the structure of this lesson incorporated their personal and family experiences in the context of Polish history of the last 60 years. The students related family stories told to them by their grandparents about World War II, and by their parents about life under communism. A class discussion about freedom related these stories to their own experiences in post-communist Poland.

ESL, EFL, and Bilingual Education: Exploring Historical, Sociocultural, Linguistic, and Instructional Foundations, pp. 153–157

Finally, groups of students created pictorial representations of freedom which they presented to the class.

OUTLINE OF THE LESSON

- **Age Level:** high school and up
- **English Level:** low-intermediate and up
- **Time Allowed:** minimum 45 minutes
- **Materials:** paper (to make a banner); colored markers and pencils

1. **Pair work—Sharing stories**
    - In pairs, tell a story that your grandparents told about World War II.
    - A few students share their stories with the class.
    - Switch pairs and tell a story that your parents told about life in Poland before 1989.
    - A few students share their stories with the class.

2. **Whole Class Discussion**
    - How are your grandparents and parents experiences similar or different?
    - How are their experiences similar to or different from your own?

3. **Freedom Discussion**
    Brainstorm—what does freedom mean?
    - Relating to the stories you told, what do you think freedom meant to your grandparents? your parents?
    - What does **freedom** mean to you?
      o Freedom to …
      o Freedom from …
    - Talk about the value of freedom—what would you exchange freedom for? Is freedom worth material possessions? Is freedom worth your life? Is freedom worth the life of another person?

4. **Representation of Freedom**
    - In groups of four, create a visual representation, using words and pictures, of what your group thinks freedom is.
    - Present this to the class.

HOW I IMPLEMENTED THE LESSON

Most of the students in camp were born in the late 1980s, so to lay the groundwork, I asked them if their grandparents had related stories about their lives in Poland during World War II. The students then talked in pairs to tell a story that a grandparent had shared about World War II. A few students shared their stories with the entire class, providing a wide range of stories.

- One girl told how her grandmother had continued her education while in hiding during the war. The priest would go from house to house teaching small groups of children away from the eyes and ears of German troops.
- Another told how her grandmother, a teenager, threw a Molotov cocktail at a German tank.
- One boy's grandfather was sent to a forced labor in camp in Germany.

After sharing a few of these stories, I then asked the students if they had heard their parents discuss their lives prior to 1989, the end of the Communist era in Poland. They switched partners and told a story that their parents had told them.

- One boy told about his father's arrest for smuggling goods into Poland.
- Several students told stories of shortages their parents suffered during this time and about the tickets they had to have in order to buy almost everything, from washing machines to beef.

After a few students had shared their stories with the class, I then led a full-class discussion.

- First, we compared the experiences of their grandparents and parents. The main similarity was that both groups experienced a lack of freedom and of material goods. The students, on the other hand, do not experience these shortages and restrictions. They have more freedom to do things and make choices about their lives than their parents and grandparents did.
- From this, we tried to define freedom, brainstorming terms and aspects of freedom.
- I then emphasized the distinction between "freedom to ..." and "freedom from ..." and we discussed these concepts in the context

of their lives and the lives of their grandparents and parents, whose concept of freedom was based more on "freedom from …," such as freedom from oppression, hunger, and so on.

- We continued the discussion talking about the value of freedom: what would you exchange freedom for? Is freedom worth material possessions, your life, the life of another? Most of the students agreed that freedom was not worth anything material. Some of them did assert that freedom was worth their own lives, that they would die for freedom. However, most of them did not believe that their freedom was worth the lives of their loved ones. They would sacrifice their freedom for the life of a loved one. Several commented that while living in freedom was preferable, it is possible to exist without freedom because your captor cannot control your mind and thoughts.

- Finally, in groups of four, the students created a pictorial representation of freedom which they presented to the class. Each group had colored markers and pencils and four sheets of fanfold paper to create banners portraying how they perceived freedom. Primarily, their pictures presented their generation' notion that freedom is "freedom to …"

DISCUSSING ABSTRACT CONCEPTS IN THE EFL CLASSROOM

Freedom is one of many abstract concepts that can be an interesting and challenging discussion topic for students in the EFL classroom. With careful planning, such an abstract concept can be framed in such a way that students can use concrete examples from their own lives and experiences to explore their thoughts and feelings about freedom.

To find an abstract concept which is relevant in the lived experiences of your students, research the history of their country for the past 50 years. This time frame is the richest because this is the period about which they have most likely heard family stories. Depending on where you are, the abstract concept which is relevant to your students may be peace/war; poverty; religion; or, even, the destruction/preservation of the environment. The discussion will be limited only by the level of your students' English skills.

REFLECTION QUESTIONS

1.   What are other topics that would lend themselves well to this type of activity?

2. How could you modify this activity for younger students or students who have a lower level of English?

3. How could you assess this assignment?

FOLLOW-UP ACTIVITIES

1. Find similar lessons and compare how they approach the concepts and what kinds of activities they use.

2. Write a content objective and a language objective for this lesson.

FURTHER READING

- Dave's ESL Café: www.eslcafe.com
- Teaching Tolerance: www.teachingtolerance.com

CHAPTER 13

LET EVERY VOICE BE HEARD

Creating Effective Groups

This lesson was created as a teacher training tool. I have presented it with variations to native English speakers who are in teacher preparation courses, as well as to English as a foreign language (EFL) teachers who teach English at the elementary and secondary levels. I have presented this lesson to a class of English teachers from China as well as in a conference workshop with English teachers from all over the world. This chapter explains the goals of the lesson and how teachers can use it to improve their skills in creating groups in their classrooms, and includes the scripted lesson plan that I have used.

INTRODUCTION

Effective group work is a form of self-directed learning which has several benefits for the learner. By placing more responsibility on the students for their learning they "gain maturity and proficiency ... they need to continually work toward becoming autonomous learners and effective communicators in the classroom and out" (Richard-Amato 2003, p. 82). For example, using group work for problem-posing helps students develop critical thinking skills not only through their own efforts but the influence

ESL, EFL, and Bilingual Education: Exploring Historical, Sociocultural, Linguistic, and Instructional Foundations, pp. 159–171
Copyright © 2010 by Information Age Publishing

of group dynamics (Wallerstein, 1983 as cited in Richard-Amato, 2003). Hedge (2000, as cited in Richard-Amato, 2003) also emphasized that such self-directed learning helps students learn how to define their own objectives, make use of language materials effectively, and organize their own learning. Besides helping students develop these skills and strategies, group work also has social and affective results. Interacting with group members effectively requires that students learn good communication strategies and skills, including self-control, and they can learn to be aware of and control their affective states (O'Malley & Chamot, 1990, as cited in Richard-Amato, 2003).

There are also practical benefits of group work. In the EFL and English as a second lanaguage (ESL) classroom it gives students the opportunity to practice their language skills more intensively using the student-student model than in the teacher-student model which is common in teacher-led activities. For ESL students in the mainstream classroom, group work can give them the opportunity to participate in a lower stress environment. Depending on the level of the student's English, and the purpose of the group, roles can be specifically designed which can ensure that the ESL student is an active part of the group. For example, if their English skills are not developed enough to be a recorder or a reporter for the group, they could be the time keeper or in charge of materials (Wong, 2005).

Group work has several purposes and you may assign your students to work in groups in class, or you may ask them to work as a group outside of class, such as for a group presentation. Regardless of the context, creating groups that engage in meaningful and effective work can be challenging in any classroom. The challenges in the EFL and ESL classroom have a few unique features involving language use, but have much in common with any type of group work situation. Several elements are essential for group work to be effective. I will discuss some of the theoretical bases of creating group activities, some of the issues that are involved, some strategies that can be used, and will offer my own suggestions.

GETTING TO KNOW ONE ANOTHER

Whether your class is in a K-12 setting or a private school for adults, groups work more effectively if students know one another, and if you know something about the students. There are any number of getting-to-know-you activities that you can use to create a group mentality among your students. You will need to accomplish this however works best in your situation. If the situation is a workshop where students will only spend a few hours together, a simple activity is sufficient. Regardless of the activity you choose, be sure that it something in which the students are learning about each other. If your students already know one another, then incorporate some kind of team building activities to develop this group mentality. Many suggestions are available on the Internet.

WHAT MAKES A GROUP SUCCEED OR FAIL?

One element that is often ignored or forgotten is that group work is not just several individuals getting together to do something. The whole is more than the sum of the parts and groups take on distinct personalities and characters. The group needs to function as a unit and accomplishing that takes some work.

The Working in Groups Guide (Appendix A) which I adapted from http://isites.harvard.edu/fs/html/icb.topic58474/wigintro.html has a good outline for students about how to organize their groups, as well as information about group dynamics and how groups functions. Also useful are the problems and solutions it offers.

Harry Wong (2005) also offers useful suggestions on how to create effective groups. I like to show the video clip of his explanation of what makes a group function well to my students who are native speakers, because he is funny and entertaining. However, I have found that he speaks rather fast for non-native speakers, so I either offer them an outline of what he is saying or I go over the information briefly without showing the video. The two elements that Wong (2005, n.d.) says are most important for groups to well are assigning roles, so that each group member has a task to do, and giving the students clear procedures. In that way students know what they need to do and how they need to do it which helps create more cohesive among the group. If they are constantly having to stop and ask the teacher what to do, they do not learn to rely on one another. The more independently the group can work, the more effective it will be.

The lesson that I created for teaching about effective group work was based on these principles. First of all, I start the groups out working a project that is doomed to failure. Then we talk about why the project failed. I lead this into a discussion about group work and groups they have participated in that were effective and that were not. We discuss some of the points on the Getting Started portion of the Working in Groups Guide. As we get to the point of talking about roles, I offer several examples of groups and elicit types of roles that they would need in this group. Depending on the class, I will then show the Harry Wong video clip or I will discuss the two major points he makes about effective group work. Then we discuss the elements of groups dynamics and why understanding them is important for having a group that functions well. Then we go through some of the items on the list of Common Problems and Solutions. Throughout all of these discussions, I encourage my students or workshop participants to relate to and reflect on their own personal experiences with group work. Finally, I assign them a group project to do that is structured and that they can be successful with generally creating poster about a topic. The topic may vary, but if this is a group of people who do not know each other, I like to have them create a poster that introduces their group. Sometimes, I may tell them that they are applying for positions at a new school as a group and they should focus on the qualities that make their group a strong group to hire. After they have completed their projects, they share them with the rest of the class. The debriefing session focuses on improving the Group Process.

MY SCRIPTED LESSON PLAN
FOR TEACHING TEACHERS ABOUT GROUP WORK

Time required: 2-3 hours
Materials needed:

- marshmallows and uncooked spaghetti (or packing peanuts, drinking straws, and toothpicks) for Tower Building Activity;
- small prizes for the winning group of Tower Builders—pencils or stickers work well;
- Working in Groups Guide handout (Appendix A);
- Harry Wong video (optional);
- Group Roles handout (Appendix B);
- Group Planning Worksheet (Appendix C); and
- Poster paper, markers and/or crayons—for final Poster Activity.

Learning objective: Participants will work in groups to create and present to the class a poster which demonstrates their understanding of their composition as a group.

Warm-up: Tower Building Activity

Give the participants the following instruction:

- Form groups of 4-5 people.

After they have formed groups (with no guidance from you), give each group a set of materials for the Tower Building Activity. Tell them:

- I have given you some materials. When I say "Go," you will have 5 minutes to build the highest free-standing tower that you can.

Do not give any further instructions, but walk around and look at progress. Remind them that the tower has to be free-standing. Throughout the five minutes call out the time about once a minute until the last minute then call out 45 seconds, 30 seconds, 15 seconds, and STOP. (Try to be a little annoying about keeping time, so that participants feel rushed.)

Give prizes to the group with highest tower.

Discuss the project, asking some or all of the following questions:

- How did this group project go?
- What went well?
- What were some problems?
- What would have made it better?
- How did you plan you project?
- Who did the work?
- Was there a leader?
- Was there someone who kept time for you? (It was you, of course. Try to elicit how annoying your behavior was so you can talk about how the time keeper should handle their role.)
- What other roles emerged?
- What are some roles that would have been helpful?

Introduction to Group Work

Discuss group work in general asking some or all of the following questions:

- In what situations do you work in groups?
- Why would you want your students to work in groups (efficiency; real world; develops social skills)?
- Have you ever worked in a group that worked well? Why did it work well?
- How about groups that haven't worked well?

Give participants the Working in Groups Guide handout:

- The handout has suggestions how to make groups function better. We will read over it and discuss how to make groups that work well. Some of the information is aimed at all groups and some of it is aimed at groups working outside of class.

Focus on these four points of the Getting Started section of the Working in Groups Guide handout

- Point 1: Why is this important?
- Point 2: What are some other ideas?
- Point 3: When would you want the same leader? Different leaders? What are the advantages/disadvantages?
- Point 4 – what are some other roles? How will you determine them?
- What roles would you need for each of the following situations?
  o Group of three to do a science experiment about photosynthesis
  o Group of 5 to design a web site about China
  o Group of 8 to create a poster introducing your group
- What is the problem with larger groups? How can you determine optimal group size?

At this point you can show the group work portion of the Harry Wong video or refer to the group work section in this file online: http://www.effectiveteaching.com/secure/uploads/file/SuccessfulTeaching.pdf

After watching the video or discussing the group work file, reinforce the points by asking:

- What are the two most important things he says to make groups function well? (Assigning roles; Clear procedures)

Overview of Roles

Give participants the sample Group Roles handout. Quickly review what is on the handout.

Introduction to Group Dynamics and Group Functioning

Focus on these points of the Group Dynamics and Group Functioning section of the Working in Groups Guide handout

- Point 1: Why is total participation important?
- Point 2: How can you break the assignment up into smaller tasks? Is it always the same for every assignment?
- Point 3: How can you help one another?
- Point 4/5: How can you work out difficulties?
- Point 6: How can you tell if the group is working well?
- Point 7: Whose responsibility is this?

Examining Group Problems and How to Solve Them

Tell the participants:

- Despite everyone's best efforts, groups don't always work well. These are some of the most common problems.

Ask participants to work in pairs and look over Some Common Problems (and Some Solutions) of the Working in Groups Guide. Loosely assign 1 or 2 of the problems/solutions to the pairs.

- Read your problem(s) and discuss whether you have experienced it(them) in a group situation. Then look at the solutions and choose one you think would be effective or suggest your own.

Ask a pair to share about each. As they share, you may one to focus on an aspect of each one:

- Floundering—what causes trouble getting started
- Dominating/reluctant participants—which are you?
- Digressions/tangents—talking off-topic—is this always bad?
- Getting stuck—too many ideas/not enough ideas
- Rush to work—are you this person?
- Ignoring or ridiculing others—how can the group handle this?

Group Project

Form groups of 4-5 participants, depending on how large your group is. Once they are situated, tell them:

- You will working in groups to create a poster which you will use to introduce your group. You will have 20 minutes (or more if you have time) to discuss, design, and create your poster. Then you will have a few minutes to present your poster. Your poster should focus on who you are as a group, not as individuals.
- What should you do first? (Decide on and assign roles)
- I have paper and markers that your materials' handler can get when you are ready.
- Hand out Group Planning Worksheet.
- Please fill this out as you plan.
- If you need to leave the room for any reason during this time, you may. (You are attempting to create a calm atmosphere, in contrast to the Tower Building Activity, so you may say whatever is appropriate at this time.)
- Give groups as much time as you can to work on their projects. Then ask them to present their posters. (If there is not time for every group to present, ask just a few.)

Debriefing: Improving the Group Process

After all presentations are made, debrief of group process.

- How did you decide on your roles?
- How did you decide who would do what?
- Were there any problems? How did you resolve them?
- What would have made this group project better?

APPENDIX A

Working in Groups Guide

Getting Started

- Introduce yourselves. Find out something about each other.
- Exchange contact information.
- Lay out some ground rules, such as how to contact one another if you cannot come to a meeting, how you will handle disagreements about the project, and so on.
- Define a leadership structure: One leader? Rotating leadership? In addition to participating as a group member, the leader has certain

responsibilities. These include organizing the work and managing the group so that there is a positive work atmosphere within the group.

- Define what other roles are needed, such as, a recorder, a time keeper, a reporter, and so on.

Group Dynamics and Group Functioning

- Groups work best when everyone realizes that the task requires everyone's cooperation and contributions. Everyone should contribute to the discussions and brainstorms. Group members must listen to one another and allow everyone's opinions and ideas to be expressed. The format of the discussion may need to be changed so that everyone can contribute.
- A large project may seem overwhelming, so breaking it into smaller parts and giving different individuals responsibility for each part can make it more manageable.
- Create a timeline which describes what will be done when by whom.
- Create a sense of shared pride and accomplishment by recognizing hard work, and everyone pitching in when things are not going well.
- When there is a disagreement or if someone is dominating the group or being left out, these issues should not be ignored. They need to be addressed directly with the understanding that even if you disagree with the group's decision, you will complete the project.
- Call in outside help when needed.
- When a group is functioning well, work is getting done, and constructive group processes are creating a positive atmosphere.
- It should be expected that not everyone contributes equally all the time.

Some Common Problems (and Solutions)

- *Floundering*: false starts, indecision, circular discussions
  o I think we are trying to accomplish ... Do we agree?
  o Let's write down our main points.
  o What do we need to move forward?
  o Let's hear everyone's suggestions about what we should do next.
- *Dominating participants and reluctant participants*: those who dominate talk too much or do not take turns appropriately. They interrupt

others and may try to wrest control of the group. This behavior can prevent others from contributing, or even intimidate them. This behavior may have to be addressed directly within or away from the group. If a person is reluctant because they are shy, they may feel more comfortable talking to the leader one-on-one away from the group.

o   Let's just state the general problem and leave the details for now.

o   Let's take turns and hear what everyone has to say before we move on.

o   Has everyone contributed? Have we heard everyone's opinion?

- *Digressions and tangents*—while it is important to explore interesting avenues of thought, they can lead the group too off-topic.

  o   We need to look at our agenda and see if we are on track.

  o   Where were we before we digressed? What were we trying to do?

  o   Do we need to re-examine the topic to see if there is something about that is making it difficult to stick to?

- *Getting stuck*—may need a short break or a change in focus.

  o   Let's see if we can better identify the problem.

  o   What is preventing us from solving this problem?

  o   Let's hear everyone's ideas about what we should do next.

  o   Shall we work at it for 15 more minutes?

- *Rush to work*—there is often person who is less patient or may be more action-oriented than other group members who may try to control the pace of the group.

  o   Is everyone ready to go with this decision?

  o   What else do we need to do before we move forward?

  o   Let's see what other ideas are out there.

- *Ignoring or ridiculing others*—when someone consistently ignores, ridicules, or criticizes others, this needs to be addressed either with a humor in the group or as a private aside outside the group.

Note: This guide was adapted from Derek Bok Center for Teaching and Learning, Harvard University. (1997).

APPENDIX B

- Group Roles
  - o **Group Facilitator/ Leader**: moderates discussions, keeps the group on task, assures work is done by all, and makes sure all have opportunity to participate and learn. May also want to check to make sure that all of the group members have mastered the learning points of a group.
  - o **Timekeeper/ Monitor**: monitors time and moves group along so that they complete the task in the available time, keeps area clean, assumes role of any missing group member if there is no wildcard member.
  - o **Recorder:** takes notes of the group's discussion and prepares a written conclusion. The recorder picks and maintains the group files and folders on a daily basis and keeps records of all group activities including the material contributed by each group member. The recorder writes out the solutions to problems for the group to use as notes or to submit to the instructor. The recorder may also prepare presentation materials when the group makes oral presentations to the class.
- **Summarizer/Clarifier**: restates the group's conclusions or answers.
- **Elaborator**: relates the discussion with prior concepts and knowledge.
- **Research-Runner:** gets needed materials and is the liaison between groups and between their group and the instructor.
- **Wildcard:** The wildcard acts as an assistant to the group leader and assumes the role of any member that may be missing.

Note: From Srinivas (n.d.).

APPENDIX C

Group Planning Worksheet

Project Name: _____ Date: _____

Time allowed for project: _____

Group Name: _____

Group Members	Roles

REFERENCES

Derek Bok Center for Teaching and Learning, Harvard University. (1997). *Working in groups: A note to faculty and a quick guide for students.* Retrieved http://isites.harvard.edu/fs/html/icb.topic58474/wigintro.html

Richard-Amato, P. (2003). *Making it happen: From interactive to participatory language teaching* (3rd ed.). White Plains, NY: Longman.

Srinivas, H. (n.d.). *Collaborative learning structures and techniques.* University of Texas, Teaching Resource Center. Retrieved from http://www.gdrc.org/kmgmt/c-learn/methods.html

Wong, H. (2005). *The effective teacher.* [DVD]. Sunnyvale, CA: Harry K. Wong Publications.

Wong, H. (n.d.) *Successful teaching: For teachers who want to be effective (91).* Retrieved from http://www.effectiveteaching.com/secure/uploads/file/SuccessfulTeaching.pdf

REFLECTION QUESTIONS

1. What were the characteristics of groups you have participated in that functioned well?
2. How would you assess group work?
3. Which aspect of group dynamics and group function is the most difficult to manage? Why?

FOLLOW-UP ACTIVITIES

1. Compare several websites for teachers that focus on group roles and group functioning. Analyze the effectiveness of the various elements and roles.
2. Observe a teacher who is using group work with his/her students. Analyze the effectiveness of the various strategies the teacher uses.

FURTHER READING

- Barbara G. Davis, Collaborative Learning: Group Work and Study Teams Tools for Teaching: http://teaching.berkeley.edu/bgd/collaborative.html
- Cooperative Learning: http://edtech.kennesaw.edu/intech/cooperativelearning.htm

CHAPTER 14

USING FREE VOLUNTARY READING IN THE ESL CLASSROOM

The chapter is based on a workshop presentation that I prepared for teachers to model how to combine the idea of *free voluntary reading* (FVR) with a *paper bag book report* (Hoff, 1998). Although the idea of the FVR as proposed by Krashen (2004) would be antithetical to tying it to such an assignment, I will justify my reasons for doing so.

WHY FVR?

According to Stephen Krashen (2004), FVR is

> reading because you want to: no book reports, no questions at the end of the chapter. In FVR, you don't have to finish the book if you don't like it. FVR is the kind of reading most of us do obsessively all the time. (p. 1)

Krashen (2004) further says that although FVR by itself will not "produce the highest levels of competence" it will provide "a foundation so that higher levels of proficiency will be reached" (p. 1).

Krashen (2004) identifies three types of in-school free-reading programs and cites research which supports his ideas:

ESL, EFL, and Bilingual Education: Exploring Historical, Sociocultural, Linguistic, and Instructional Foundations, pp. 173–178
Copyright © 2010 by Information Age Publishing

- Sustained silent reading (SSR): teachers and students read 5-15 minutes/day;
- Self-selected reading: free reading is a large part of the language arts program—teachers and students have conferences about what the students have read; and
- Extensive reading: students only give a short summary of what was read.

In looking at research which examines the impact of FVR, Krashen (2004) found that "In-school free reading programs are consistently effective" (p. 2) for English speakers as well as for second language learners.

- Improves literacy growth;
- Increased reading comprehension (McNeil, 1976);
- Pleasant—creates a low anxiety environment;
- Results in superior general knowledge;
- Improved vocabulary development, grammar performance, writing, oral/aural language (Greaney, 1970; Krashen, 1989);
- Improved spelling (Collins, 1980; Hafiz and Tudor, 1990; Elley, 1991); and
- Higher Test of English as a Foreign Language (TOEFL) scores (Constantino, Lee, Cho, & Krashen, 1997; Gradman & Hanania, 1991).

One of the premises of FVR is that there are no book reports—it is just what is says, free reading. I agree with Krashen that students should be encouraged to read for the sake of reading. I love to read and cannot imagine not wanting to sit with a good book or even a cereal box and not wanting to devour the contents, metaphorically speaking, of course. However, I also know that in the school year, time is important and that students need to learn other skills.

My decision is also supported by evidence from the work of psychologists Jean Piaget, Lev Vygotsky, and Michael Halliday (Robb, 1994), who believed that learning language and solving problems are active social events. They also asserted that learners comprehend how language works by using it. This lesson which combines reading for pleasure and sharing that reading with others meets the criteria of an active social language event.

Therefore, I am proposing that the paper bag book report (Hoff, 1998) be used as a fun way to introduce students to book report writing. Students will have the freedom to choose their own book, and will have ample time to complete the project. Designing a creative and fun book report based on a book that was freely chosen will be an effective method of encouraging reading and developing the skills needed to prepare more complex oral and written reports.

I have written a description of the lesson, then rather than writing this activity as a lesson plan, I have included relevant parts of the script that I used for the 30-minute workshop. The italicized parts indicated the teacher's voice.

COMBINING FVR AND THE PAPER BAG BOOK REPORT

The goal of this project is for students to read and talk about a book that they chose independently. They will support their talk with a visual aid they have created using a paper bag. This project would be suitable for any age or grade-level student.

The teacher could introduce the project by first leading a discussion about a book they had recently finished reading as a class. Depending on the level of the students and their English proficiency the teacher and students could talk about characters in the book, the plot, themes, and so on.

Then the teacher should model what the students are supposed to do. In my workshop presentation, I assumed that the students were middle school to high school age, so I chose the book *Holes* by Louis Sachar (1999). After the teacher models using his/her brown bag, then he/she can offer the students some suggestions for books to read. The teacher may have an in-class library they can choose from. However, I suggest that he/she can solicit the assistance of the school library media specialist. The class could go to the library or the media specialist could collect an assortment of books to bring to your class. He/she could then give a brief book talk about each book, giving the students a chance to look them over and make their selections. The teacher could supply students with brown paper lunch-bag size bags so that everyone would have access to the same kind of bag.

WORKSHOP SCRIPT

I held up my book, *Holes*.

- Has anyone read this book?
- *Look at the cover. What can we tell about this book?*
- *Title—what do you think it's about?—What is the gold seal? Who remembers?*

- *This book was a Newbery winner, an award given to young adult books by the American Library Association. So they thought this was a pretty good book, and I agree.*
- After you read your book and think about it, you are going to tell the class about it, and I am going to show you how now.

Then I held up a paper bag which has holes cut in it..

- *This paper bag has all the information that I need to tell you about my book. What is the first thing you notice about my bag?*
- *Holes, that's right. The name of my book is* Holes, *by Louis Sachar.*
- *There are some things in my bag. Let's see what I have.*

  o **Stanley's name** (I printed Stanley Yelnats on both sides of a strip of paper so they could see how it was a palindrome)

- *Stanley Yelnats is overweight and he is unpopular. Stanley's family has never had any luck ever since great-great-grandfather stole a pig. Stanley has been sent to Camp Green Lake, Texas, a boy's detention facility for a crime he did not commit. The lake is long gone, and all that remains is a dry lake bed.*

  o **Bottle of sand**

- *The camp is run by Mr. Pendanski—a camp counselor, Mr. Sir—the sadistic, sunflower-eating guard,*

  o **Sunflower seeds**

- *and the mysterious Warden who runs the camp with her own unique set of rules. Stanley is assigned to Tent D which he shares with other boys nicknamed Squid, X-Ray, Zero, Magnet, Armpit, and ZigZag.*

  o **A spoon (representing a shovel)**

- *Every day in the blistering heat, the boys are required to dig a hole--5 feet deep, and 5 feet wide. At first, Stanley thinks this is some sort of senseless requirement to keep the boys busy, but it occurs to him that they are actually digging for something—something extremely important, and Stanley is right.*

  o **Tube of lipstick**

- *When one of the boy's finds a tube of lipstick, the warden becomes very excited. No one knows yet, but this lipstick belonged to Kissin' Kate Barlow, an outlaw who kissed all the men she robbed and murdered.*

- *Stanley undergoes a miraculous change as the story progresses. Not only does he change physically (thanks to digging all those holes), but mentally too. Stanley learns the true value of friendship and loyalty through his relationship with fellow inmate, Zero, and it is through this relationship that Stanley matures.*

- *One of the things I really liked about this book is that everything connects to something else. Like the holes—they are continuous. Stanley's family's problems started because of Kissin' Kate Barlow and ended because of her. This theme of connections is part of what makes it so interesting.*

- *Does this sound like a book you would like to read? I recommend it. It is funny and sad and serious all at the same time.*

- *As you are reading your book, you will need to think about what you will put in your paper bag. You may choose to read any book you want. I have a few here that I'd like to suggest that you look at.*

REFERENCES

Hoff, C. (1998). Paper bag book reports. *Educator's Reference Desk*. Retrieved from http://www.eduref.org/Virtual/Lessons/Language_Arts/Reading/RDG0011.html

Krashen, S. (2004). *The power of reading: Insights from the research* (2nd ed.). Portsmouth, NH: Libraries Unlimited.

Robb, L. (1994). *Whole language, whole learners: Creating a literature-centered classroom*. New York, NY: William Morrow and Company.

Sachar, L. (1999). *Holes*. New York, NY: Random House.

REFLECTION QUESTIONS

1. Do you enjoy reading? Why? Why not?
2. Krashen claims that reading is the key to good writing. What do you think?
3. Why would you implement FVR in your classroom?

FOLLOW-UP ACTIVITIES

1. Compare research studies on the effectiveness of programs such as DEAR, FVR, and SSR. Do they agree with Krashen?

2. Find other lessons that you could use to stimulate students' interest in reading. Compare the strategies each use and reflect on the effectiveness of each.

FURTHER READING

*   Gunderson, L. (2008). *ESL (ELL) literacy instruction: A guidebook to theory and practice* (2nd ed.). New York: NY Routledge.
*   Szendeffy, J. (1997). *For here or to go?: An ESL reader.* Ann Arbor, MI: University of Michigan Press.

CHAPTER 15

THE SCHOOL LIBRARY
AND THE ESL STUDENT

INTRODUCTION

Many students in American schools are expected to perform in a situation that is more stressful than most educators can imagine. Imagine walking into work every morning and no one greeting you or smiling at you. Imagine that when someone does finally speak to you, they mispronounce your name. Then imagine that this person asks you a question and then frowns when you try to tell them that you do not understand. Then imagine someone talking to you for 45 minutes and, despite all your concentration, you have understood about one third of what was said, then they tell you that you will have a 25 question multiple choice test on this information tomorrow. This is what English speakers of other languages (ESOL) students go through every day.

Schools around the country are teaching more and more students whose first language is not English. The National Center for English Language Acquisition (2007), reports that as of the 2006-2006 school year, 5 million of the 49.3 million children attending public school were non-English speaking. That is an increase of 57.1% since 1996. There are several terms used for students who do not speak English as their first language. They may be called language minority students. They may be ESL (English as a second language) students. Some programs refer to them as

ESL, EFL, and Bilingual Education: Exploring Historical, Sociocultural, Linguistic, and Instructional Foundations, pp. 179–185

LEP (limited English proficiency) or ESOL (English speakers of other Languages). Whatever term is used, these students all have one thing in common: English is not their first language, and, generally, it is not the language they and their families speak at home.

These students may come from a variety of cultures and backgrounds. Their academic skills and abilities, like any other population of students, vary widely. Some learn easily; others do not. An added dimension to the learning of ESOL students is that in addition to general learning skills and abilities, they come to school with a wide variety of English language skills.

As the diversity in American communities grows, the school community is evolving to provide opportunities for learning that support an environment in which all students can grow. Efforts are being made by school systems to ensure that these students receive the best possible education by providing them with the materials and teachers that they need to be academically successful. Specially trained English language teachers provide the students with English language skills, while teachers in all classes are learning how to employ modifications that will make learning in subject areas easier and less stressful for these students. The school library media specialist can play a pivotal role in developing positive learning experiences for these students by providing appropriate reading materials, fiction and nonfiction, as well as research-oriented and instructional software. The media specialist can also help teachers design instructional programs that are relevant for this group of students.

After introducing some general guidelines for working with ESOL students, I will present four ways in which the media specialist can help meet the needs of this population. These suggestions are based on my own experiences as a high school media specialist.

GENERAL GUIDELINES FOR WORKING WITH ESOL STUDENTS

One of the most important actions that any teacher can take when working with ESOL students is to help the students relax. This is best accomplished by daily one-on-one interaction with the student. The media specialist may not see these students every day, but she/he will interact with these students either through their mainstream classes or in their ESOL classes on numerous occasions. In these interchanges, the media specialist may need to make an extra effort to be sure that the ESOL students feel relaxed in their trip to the media center. A smile can work wonders.

Another important technique that educators can use is to make the material more accessible to the students. This may mean preparing a handout, so the student can follow along as explanations are made. Explanations should use simple, clear language, high-lighting key concepts. Materials should be provided that are appropriate for these students' reading levels. This can easily be done when these students make trips to the media center if the media specialist and teachers plan together and the teacher alerts the media specialist to any special needs in his/her class.

WHAT THE MEDIA SPECIALIST CAN DO

There are four areas in which the media specialist can help ESOL students. First, a media center orientation just for ESOL classes can be an effective way to introduce students to the media center and its staff, as well as to the materials housed in the media center. Second, collection development should be done with this population in mind. Third, book talks geared to these students can help make leisure reading more pleasurable. Last, research skills can be taught with modifications to these students so that the research process seems less overwhelming.

Media Center Orientation

Early in the school year, the media specialist should plan a visit for the ESOL classes in the media center. This is especially important for those students who are new to the school, but can be useful for returning students, too. They may have forgotten or never understood about some of the resources available there.

During this visit, the media specialist should introduce her/himself and the other media staff, so that the students will be able to call you by name. Depending on the size of the class, and your memory, learn the names of some of the students. Like any other orientation visit, resources should be shown to the students, but not too many and not with too much information. Show them where the reference books and encyclopedias are; where fiction is shelved; where nonfiction is shelved; and where there are computers they can use for Internet searching or for CD-ROM searches. Do not give them detailed instructions at this point on how to use these materials. That can be done on subsequent visits. Prepare a simple activity that allows them to locate and look at some of the materials. A scavenger hunt with a map of the library with sections clearly labeled can be a fun activity. As the students are leaving, smile at them and call several of them by name. You are well on your way to making visits to the media center more enjoyable for these students.

Collection Development

ESOL teachers often have a list of materials that they would like for their students to have access to. Before placing your book order, consult with her or him. There may be novice students (those who speak little or no English) who would benefit from some type of picture books that the high school media specialist would normally never consider ordering. The teacher may have a suggested reading list for the students to use as their entrance into leisure reading in English. There may be certain reference materials, such as picture dictionaries, that the ESOL teacher would like to have available for the students. Audio books of some popular titles or of titles used in their mainstream classes might be helpful for students whose listening skills are more developed than their reading skills.

An article in *Library Journal* (Hansen, Barabino, & Floyd, 1992) advises:

> Before adding a title to an ESL collection, the selector should consider the book's applicability, along with the usual concerns of quality, authority, and presentation. Is the book for a learner literate in his or her own language? What is its understanding, speaking, reading, and writing level? What learning method and teaching approach is the book compatible with? Does it support the philosophy and methodology of your ESL program? Is it vivid and exciting enough to assure that today's learners enjoy it and won't fall asleep? If it is for self-teaching, does it offer enough support? These are the important questions in ESL. The librarian can also add books not specifically designed to teach but which add literary and cultural integrity, thus increasing the impact of the ESL collection for students and teachers. (p. 140)

You may even consider buying some books in the students' home languages or that are bilingual. Students will appreciate the opportunity to enjoy occasional reading in a language they are competent in and feel comfortable with. It is important so that they not forget that reading can be an enjoyable experience.

Book Talks

Book talks are very effective with this group of students. They are often overwhelmed by the amount of English they are being exposed to. Introducing books with short book talks can help them focus on a certain book rather having to try to choose from many. They may be done in the media center or in the ESOL classroom. Both ways are effective. The advantage to doing it in the classroom is that there are fewer distractions for the students and they are presented with a limited number of choices reducing the stress of selection for them.

When doing a book talk with ESOL students, speak slowly and clearly, not more loudly. Use simple language to convey the plot and main features of the book. Do not spend more than 2-3 minutes on each book. Watch the students' faces for incomprehension. The ESOL teacher may even be able to smooth the process by helping explain unfamiliar vocabulary. One of the books I had chosen to book talk was a low-level, high-interest book with an architect as the main character. The teacher spent a few moments checking that the students knew the term and that it was connected with "building," a word they had learned in a recent lesson, then I continued the book talk.

Another time, we had to reschedule a trip to the media center for book check-out and I was unable to be there to do a book talk. Instead, I provided an annotated reading list for the students to look at before their trip to the media center.

Teaching Research Skills to ESOL Students

Library research projects can be a daunting task for any student, but much more so for the ESOL student who has not been properly prepared. A planning session with the ESOL teacher can help the media specialist and the teacher prepare a rewarding research experience for the students. The following examples are two research projects that a high school ESOL teacher and I planned and worked on together.

As a first research project, the students were required to put together a booklet about their country of origin. The teacher and I divided the research into three sections: print encyclopedia, CD-ROM encyclopedia, and MacGlobe, a geography program available in the computer lab. The advantages to working with these students in this way were that I was able to take my time explaining how to use the various materials and I was able to give individual attention to the students who needed it.

During the first visit to the media center, I talked to the students a bit about their project and the kinds of information they would be seeking. Then we looked at encyclopedias and their organization. The students found their countries in the appropriate volume of the encyclopedia and began taking notes. The ESOL teacher had already been working with the students in class on note-taking skills.

The next visit, the students learned how to access the CD-ROM encyclopedias: Grolier's and Encarta. They used these sources to add to the information that had already gathered. Scanning for information was stressed in this part of the research process.

For the final visit to the media center, we went into the computer lab and the students learned to use MacGlobe. MacGlobe has some specific statistical information which is in an easily understood format, such as graphs of population statistics, and tables of economic resources.

As a final part of this project, I gave the students discarded magazines to cut up for pictures to illustrate their booklets. Those who did not have computers at home were scheduled into the lab for word processing. As a final service, I bound the students' booklets into one large booklet for each class. I prepared a nice cover with each student's name and country on the front and displayed the bound books in the media center for a few days. The students were justifiably proud of their efforts.

A second research project that the ESOL students did later in the year was to write a short biography of a famous person and create a poster using this information. This project enabled them to use some of the resources they had learned about when doing the first project, and I introduced them to Internet searching as a new piece. I showed them how to access *Encyclopedia Britannica Online*, as well as how to search using several search engines.

One student in the advanced ESOL section, Betsy, wanted to research a popular Latin American model. When I saw her topic, I told her that she might not be able to find enough information. Betsy insisted that she be allowed to do what she wanted because "you teachers just want us to learn about old dead people." I tried to explain that we were just trying to be sure that she had a successful project and she insisted that she would. A week or so later, I was in the ESOL classroom to deliver some materials when the teacher was collecting the projects. I saw a really nice poster about Mahatma Gandhi and could not remember who had researched him. I looked at the back of the poster and there was Betsy's name.

CONCLUSION

It is easy to overlook ESOL students as a group that can benefit from visits as a class to the media center. Since the students are usually in mainstream classes, they often make visits to the media center with these classes. However, they can benefit from visits designed for them as ESOL students. They often do not pick up everything that is going on in the mainstream classroom. By working with these students in their ESOL class, they can receive more individualized instruction, as the classes are generally smaller and they are often more comfortable with this group. The next time these students come to the media center with a mainstream class, they will not be as intimidated by the process. A benefit for the media specialist is that the students learn to trust the media specialist and can become some of your most faithful patrons and your friends.

REFERENCES

Hansen, J., Barabino, D., & Floyd, D. (1992). English without tears: ESL materials. *Library Journal, 117*(9), 139-142.

The National Center for English Language Acquisition. (2007). The Growing Numbers of Limited English Proficient Students: 1995/96-2005-06. *National Clearinghouse for English Language Acquisition.* Retrieved from www.ncela.gwu.edu/files/uploads/4/GrowingLEP_0506.pdf

REFLECTION QUESTIONS

1. What are some other ways the school librarian can work with ESOL students?
2. How can lessons be planned so that library skills can be integrated into the plan?
3. What are some advantages and disadvantages of an in-class library for ESOL students?

FOLLOW-UP ACTIVITIES

1. Interview a school librarian about what materials they have available for ESOL students.
2. Plan a lesson that integrates library skills.

FURTHER READING

- Dame, M. (2003). *Serving linguistically and culturally diverse students: Strategies for the school librarian.* Retrieved from http://www.libraryinstruction.com/diversity.html
- Kathy Schrock's Guide for Educators: http://school.discoveryeducation.com/schrockguide

CHAPTER 16

TEACHING ABOUT PREJUDICE USING YOUTUBE

Meeting Language and Content Objectives

Abstract concepts can be interesting and challenging discussion topics for students in ESL/EFL classrooms. However, these concepts can be difficult to discuss effectively without proper preparation and structure. Taking advantage of the wide variety of material from YouTube and other similar websites such as TeacherTube can help you create lessons that provide the needed structure while engaging different learning styles and addressing the four skill areas of language learning.

MULTIPLE INTELLIGENCES AND THE FOUR SKILLS AREA OF LANGUAGE LEARNING

First, let's briefly review multiple intelligences, then we will examine their connections to teaching language. In the early 1980s, Howard Gardner published a ground-breaking book called *Frames of Mind* (1983) in which he suggested that intelligence is not limited only to the modalities that are measured by traditional IQ tests. He contended that people have a variety of ways of learning, not just the two or four that early researchers

ESL, EFL, and Bilingual Education: Exploring Historical, Sociocultural, Linguistic, and Instructional Foundations, pp. 187–195
Copyright © 2010 by Information Age Publishing

and educators had identified. He identified seven intelligences—seven ways that people learn and know, what we now know as multiple intelligences. Some of these intelligences were like what had already been identified—visual and auditory, but he went further and said that people also learn musically, kinesthetically, spatially, and so on. He does not claim that a person only learns one way. He says that we learn all of these ways, but one or two ways of learning may be dominant. Although his work has its critics, with continued research, the idea has expanded and grown, so that now eight and, possibly, more intelligences have been identified (see Table 20.1). The existential intelligence is added to some lists because it meets many of Gardner's criteria, but he is undecided about how it fits into the scheme. A spiritual intelligence and a moral intelligence have also been posited by Gardner, but because of the difficulty in quantifying their characteristics, he is hesitant to add them to the list.

If we take students' ways of learning into account, we need to consider using a variety of strategies and techniques to promote learning (Beare, n.d.; Palmberg, n.d.). Considering the four skill areas of language learning, reading, writing, speaking, and listening, we can see some obvious connections between multiple intelligences and these skill areas. A student's preferred intelligence or way of learning will also be linked to the skill area in which they tend to make the fastest progress. For example, a student who is strongly interpersonal will tend to focus on developing speaking skills so they can communicate. A student who is more intrapersonal may develop reading or writing skills more quickly.

YouTube can play a role in connecting to these ways of learning and to developing. It is useful especially when thinking about verbal/linguistic, visual/spatial, musical and interpersonal learning styles. However,

Table 20.1.   Multiple Intelligences

Type of Intelligence	Description
Verbal/linguistic	Words
Logical/mathematical	Reasoning and numbers
Visual/spatial	Spatial visualization
Bodily/kinesthetic	Physical
Musical	Rhythmic
Interpersonal	Social
Intrapersonal	Self-reflective
Naturalist	Natural world experience
Existential	Questioning

Source: Gardner (1983, 2006).

depending on how you use it and what you use, it could conceivably be used with the other intelligences. I can imagine using a YouTube video and students following directions for movements, incorporating the bodily/kinesthetic intelligence, and so on.

USING YOUTUBE

One useful feature of YouTube (www.youtube.com) is that it is searchable which makes finding appropriate materials a little easier. However, keep in mind that anybody and everybody can upload their videos there, so you will have to carefully preview any that you intend to use. If you do not have an Internet connection in your classroom or if your school's filtering system blocks YouTube, you may be able to download some of the videos and show them from your desktop. The final activity I will discuss is from TeacherTube (www.teachertube.com) which should be allowed through your school's filtering system. It does not have the wide range of videos available that YouTube does, but they are more focused on educational topics. Like YouTube, TeacherTube is searchable.

Carefully Taught

The first clip to look at is the song "Carefully Taught" sung by Mandy Patinkin at http://www.youtube.com/watch?v=nHKzn8aHyXg. I chose this particular version because the audio was clearer than some others. Because he is just singing and not "acting," it's also easier to focus on the lyrics. This is a song from the musical *South Pacific*. *South Pacific* takes place on a Pacific island during World War II and, besides being a love story, it explores the issue of racial prejudice. I adapted the lesson from the Teaching American History Project which can be used an introductory lesson about prejudice.

First, you would do some kind of warm up. A review of emotion words or rhyming words would make a good introduction, but what you choose will depend on the level of your students, and what you would like to focus on.

Next explain that they are going to listen to a short song called "Carefully Taught" from the musical *South Pacific* and tell them a little about the background of the story. Listen to the song once through. Then give them the handout (Appendix A) and tell them to circle the word they hear. Depending on the level of your students, you may need to play it another time. Then ask students to volunteer to read each line with the correct word. Elicit and explain meaning as needed.

The next discussion portion of the lesson will be shaped by the level and proficiency of your students. Ask the students what this song is about? You may define and elaborate as you see fit. According to the song where does prejudice come from? You may ask students to circle this information everywhere it appears in the song. Ask them to discuss whether they agree or disagree with the song, and why or why not?

As a follow-up you can do a variety of activities, again depending on the level of your students. Below are a few suggestions:

- A guided discussion about prejudice;
- Write about an example of prejudice they have seen or experienced;
- Draw a picture of prejudice and explain it; and
- Develop a skit or role play about an act of prejudice.

This song activity used music to convey a powerful message, therefore focusing on the musical intelligence. By using rhyming words it also focuses on the verbal-linguistic intelligence. Circling the words and phrases uses the kinesthetic intelligence. It also incorporates listening skills as well a little reading, some speaking, and maybe some writing, depending on how you follow up.

Prejudice

The next example is a bit different. To warm up, play a few rounds of Hangman with your students ending with the word prejudice. Elicit the definition of prejudice then show the video at

- http://www.youtube.com/watch?v=efuxiRnsOwU&feature=related (Stant0407, 2007).

This video lends itself to vocabulary building (although I would explain to students that antilocution is not a commonly used word. Perhaps you can brainstorm other words to use in its place, such as insults, or hateful speech.). A word scramble is one vocabulary activity you can use with vocabulary introduced in the clip. Another vocabulary activity you could do with this video is matching terms related to prejudice with definitions. Below is a suggested list of words:

- *Bias*: favoring one thing/group/person over another, usually unfairly;

- *Discrimination*: Unequal treatment of people based on their group membership;
- *Generalization*: a simple or general way of describing something or someone;
- *Open-minded*: open to new ideas and new people;
- *Prejudice*: An irrational and inflexible opinion formed on the basis of limited knowledge;
- *Stereotypes*: an unverified and oversimplified generalization of an entire group of people;
- *Tolerance*: being fair towards and accepting of other people's beliefs or opinions;
- *Xenophobia:* fear or hatred of foreigners;
- *Ethnocentrism*: the belief that one culture, one way of thinking and acting is superior;
- *Racism*: based on the perception that one race is superior to others; and
- *Sexism*: based on the perception that one gender is superior.

These words can be compared and contrasted. They could also be used to show a progression, as is done in the video, from generalizations to discrimination.

You would also want to have a discussion with your students. Here is an example discussion:

- Should they have used a stick man? Would another figure been as effective?
- Where might prejudice start? Why might it start? Does it always have to end in violence? What can you do to stop it?
- How do you think stick man might have felt when he was joked about? Avoided? Discriminated against? Physically attacked?
- What could have been done at each step to stop it?

In this particular group of questions, I purposefully used high-level modals to incorporate grammar into the lesson. As a follow-up activity, students could use the final question to write about or create a skit about a similar situation which explains how to stop such actions.

This video clip used visual cues to convey the message. Follow-up activities can focus in on any and all of the skills areas, as well as the verbal-linguistic intelligence, the kinesthetic intelligence, the visual spatial intelligence, for example, depending on how these activities are structured.

I Have a Dream

You can connect a history lesson with prejudice by teaching about Martin Luther King. You can give them a text about King (Appendix B) and use is as an introductory reading activity. Then you can show this abbreviated clip of his "I Have a Dream" speech at www.teachertube.com. You can use the search terms "prejudice mlk" and you can link to it or enter the url:

- http://www.teachertube.com/viewVideo.php?video_id= 71471&
  title=MLK__B_DAY (Peel, 2009).

Students can underline what they hear on the handout or you could prepare another type of listening activity for them, such as a Cloze activity. As you discuss the issues he brings up in his speech you can talk about what prejudice he and Black people faced historically and what kinds of prejudices people face today. You may ask them to write a three- or four-sentence summary of the passage giving the main ideas of the passage.

There are a wide range of follow-up activities you can do with this, depending on the level and proficiency of your students. While the focal point of this clip is listening skills, follow-up activities can incorporate all the skill areas, as well as wide range of multiple intelligences. Some suggestions are:

- Conduct research about the Civil Rights Movement or King;
- Create a timeline of the Civil Rights Movement;
- Write about their own dreams; or
- Create a mobile by making clouds from construction paper. Students can write their dreams on the clouds and then hang them from a clothes hanger to make a mobile.

CONCLUSION

Prejudice is one of many abstract concepts that can be an interesting and challenging discussion topic for students in the EFL classroom. With careful planning, such an abstract concept can be framed in such a way that students can use concrete examples from their own lives and experiences to explore their thoughts and feelings about prejudice. YouTube can provide the ESL teacher with a variety of materials to use to create lessons that address a variety of skill and learning styles. The level of engagement will be limited only by the level of your students' English skills.

APPENDIX A

Introductory Lesson on Prejudice from Jeanne Benoit
(http://www.eastconn.org/tah/IntroductoryLessonOnPrejudice.pdf)

Carefully Taught

As you listen to the song *Carefully Taught* from the Broadway Musical **South Pacific** circle the correct word.

- You've got to be taught to (date, hate) and (fear, hear)
- You've got to be taught from (dear, year) to (fear, year)
- It's got to be drummed in your dear little (dear, ear)
- You've got to be carefully taught.
- You've got to be taught to be (afraid, raid)
- Of people whose (lies, eyes) are oddly (laid, made)
- And people whose (thin, skin) is a different (shade, fade)
- You've got to be carefully taught.
- You've got to be taught before it's too (date, late)
- Before you are (sticks, six) or (heaven, seven) or (fate, eight)
- To (date, hate) all the people your relatives (fate, hate)
- You've got to be carefully taught!
- You've got to be carefully taught!

Discussion Questions

- Where does prejudice come from?
- Where do we get prejudice?
- Do you agree or disagree with the song? Explain your answer.

APPENDIX B

Excerpts from Rev. Martin Luther King's "I Have a Dream" Speech
(http://www.teachertube.com/viewVideo.php?video_id=71471
&title=MLK__B_DAY)

I have a dream that one day on the red hills of Georgia, the sons of former slaves and the sons of former slave owners will be able to sit down together at the table of brotherhood.

I have a dream my four little children will one day live in a nation where they will not be judged by the color of their skin but by the content of their character.

I have a dream today!

One day right there in Alabama little black boys and black girls will be able to join hands with little white boys and white girls as sisters and brothers.

I have a dream today!

When we allow freedom ring, when we let it ring from every village and every hamlet, from every state and every city, we will be able to speed up that day when all of God's children, black men and white men, Jews and Gentiles, Protestants and Catholics, will be able to join hands and sing in the words of the old Negro spiritual:

Free at last! Free at last! Thank God Almighty, we are free at last!

REFERENCES

Beare, K. (n.d.). *Multiple intelligences in the ESL classroom.* Retrieved from http://esl.about.com/od/teachingenglish/a/l_multiple.htm

Benoit, J. (n.d.). *Teaching American History Project, Introductory lesson on prejudice from Jeanne Benoit.* Retrieved from http://www.eastconn.org/tah/IntroductoryLessonOnPrejudice.pdf

Gardner, H. (1983). *Frames of mind: The theory of multiple intelligences.* New York, NY: Basic Books.

Gardner, H. (2006). *Multiple intelligences: New horizons in theory and practice.* New York, NY: Basic Books.

Palmberg, R. (n.d.). Catering to multiple intelligences: A foreign language lesson plan involving houses. *TEFL.net.* Retrieved from http://www.tefl.net/esl-lesson-plans/multiple-intelligences.htm

Patinkin, M. (n.d.). *Carefully taught.* Retrieved from http://www.youtube.com/watch?v=nHKzn8aHyXg

Peel, D. (2009). *I have a dream: The journey continues.* Retrieved from http://www.teachertube.com/viewVideo.php?video_id=71471&title=MLK__B_DAY

Stant0407. (2007). *Prejudice is wrong: The whos and whats.* Retrieved from http://www.youtube.com/watch?v=efuxiRnsOwU&feature=related

REFLECTION QUESTIONS

1. How have you used YouTube personally and in classes?
2. What do you think would be your biggest challenge in creating such a project?
3. How would you structure such an assignment?

FOLLOW-UP ACTIVITIES

1. Compare several YouTube sites about the same topic and analyze the strengths and weaknesses of each. Which one would you use for a class project? Why?
2. Select a lesson that you would like to teach and explore Teacher-Tube for useful footage.

FURTHER READING

- Free Documentary Films. (2009). www.freedocumentaries.com
- EFL/ESL Listening Exercises from English Online France: http://eolf.univ-fcomte.fr/index.php?page=english-listening-exercises

ABOUT THE AUTHOR

Lynn W. Zimmerman is an associate professor of education at Purdue University Calumet in Hammond, IN.

LaVergne, TN USA
30 July 2010
191420LV00002B/42/P